THE GREAT RETIREMENT MYSTERY

How To Avoid The Six Biggest Blunders

KELLEY SLAUGHT

Printed in the United States of America.

The opinions expressed are not intended to be a recommendation or investment advice and do not constitute a solicitation to buy, sell or hold a security or an investment strategy. The views and opinions expressed in this book are for information and educational purposes only.

The views and opinions in this book are those of the author at the time of writing this book, and do not reflect the opinions of [the publisher] or its editors.

Neither the publisher nor the author is engaged in rendering legal or other professional services through this book. If expert assistance is required, the services of appropriate professionals should be sought. The publisher and the author shall have neither liability nor responsibility to any person or entity with respect to any loss or damage caused directly or indirectly by the information in this publication.

The MAS Proprietary Process™ is a pending trademark of Kelley Slaught.

ISBN: 978-1-7378689-0-3

Dedication

I dedicate this book to the true loves of my life: Hayden, Shannon, and Evelyn. I love you to the moon and back.

CONTENTS

PART I

Successful Retirement Leaves Clues

Invest
STOCK
SHARES
PORTFOLIO
PROFIT

1

Why Retirement Can Be a Mystery

Like many people in the United States, you have an awesome responsibility.

Thousands of Americans are reaching the once-magical age of sixty-five each day. Retirement soon may or may not be in the cards for them.

Many questions come to mind for those approaching retirement. Can they afford to? Do they want to? Will longer and longer lifespans and inflation overwhelm their life savings? When should they choose to take Social Security? If long-term-care policies are not available, can they create a substitute?

Retirement Is A Great Mystery We Have Not Yet Faced

It is no wonder that this book is called *The Great Retirement Mystery*. Retirement is a major adjustment, going from what is called the accumulation stage of life (saving up money for later) to the spending stage (living off the savings and hoping the dollars will last). Retirement is a process most of us have never done before. It is complicated and where do we turn?

I'm Kelley Slaught and I'm here to help. I am the owner and principal of Californiawealthadvisors.com, an independent retirement/wealth advisor. I bring a unique perspective to my job. I have "retired," taking a twenty-five-year timeout to raise three children from the beginning of my financial career, and then came back to the financial advising industry.

If you are discouraged about where you stand entering the mystery of retirement, I bring an upbeat perspective to what we can do together. My motto: "There's always something to be bullish about."

Helping people retire and live well is what I do for a living. I am truly blessed to be able to do what I love, helping people. "Yes, you can retire." What a pleasure it is to tell people those reassuring words. How exciting it is for clients to hear them.

I have a philosophy behind my approach. Each individual is different and deserves a customized retirement plan of his or her own. Prepackaged or one-size-fits-all plans are like taking jigsaw puzzle pieces and pounding them to fit into the wrong holes. That may be acceptable at some large brokerages, but we refuse to do business that way.

As an independent broker, I am freed up to spend my time with clients while farming out back-office services such as recordkeeping and computerized searches.

This book is not your typical book on retirement planning. This book is my published manifesto, a public declaration of my motives and intentions to help as many people as possible achieve something of great importance: a happy and successful retirement. In these pages I do not recommend specific financial products or services. Instead, I explain a philosophy that takes the mystery out of retirement planning.

Times Have Changed

This is not your grandfather's retirement. Social Security may not have existed then. It certainly was not being taxed. Your parents worked in an era when it was fairly common to spend a career at one employer and find a pension waiting at the end. Today, pensions have all but vanished and we are encouraged to fund our own retirement accounts, sometimes with an employer match.

Some 10,000 Baby Boomers, the demographic cohort born from 1946 to 1964, are turning sixty-five each day. That is easy for demographers, including those at AARP, to project.[1]

But not all are retiring then, however. Pew Research Center calculates that only 5,900 of the 10,000 are retiring when they reach sixty-five. In fact, a much larger proportion of Baby Boomers, 51 percent, is choosing to continue work than either the Greatest Generation or the Silent Generation at comparable ages.[2]

The flip side is that many in today's workforce will be forced into early retirement by layoffs or declining health years before they expected.

After I sit down with getting-to-know-you interviews aided by a questionnaire that matches hopes and aspirations with people's assets, I craft a just-for-you retirement plan to see if they match. Sometimes clients want a part-time job for the socialization and extra income to face the future.

You have never done this before. Relax. I have more than 500 clients I help solve the mystery of retirement. Every retirement mystery is unique. The information in this book can help you crack the code for your retirement.

How Successful Retirements Begin

Some companies mark the retirement of a veteran employee with a luncheon with a few of their colleagues, or punch and cookies and time to mingle with others. An inscribed watch or plaque may symbolically mark the moment when the end of work meets the beginning of leisure time.

In reality, successful retirements begin years before. First come the decisions on how much to have withheld from paychecks for later, and how best to make that money grow. Later come the discussions with spouse and family on what we want to do on a seemingly far-off date. As it gets closer, aggressive catch-up contributions to retirement accounts may be in order.

In the coming pages, I will acquaint you with concepts to take some of the mystery out of what is ahead. I will describe some of the frequently made mistakes so that you can avoid them. There is a myriad of new products and I will provide guidance on how to decide if they may be right for you.

In what I call "cracking the code" of the retirement mystery, I outline my MAS Proprietary Process. It divides your assets into three separate sectors of about 30 percent each to diversify and reduce risk. Life throws us unexpected challenges and the remaining 10 percent is kept as an emergency reserve. Some clients perk up the moment they realize this approach means they do not have to put all their money at risk in the stock market.

Annuities come in all forms nowadays, some that allow your money to grow while protecting you from any loss of principal. I am happy to explain them and help you decide whether you feel they are right for you. Remember, annuities are not "good" or "bad." It will depend on what's right for *you*.

A retirement plan is a guide, a road map to navigate the course ahead. Sticking to the plan is so important to avoid panicked decisions when storm clouds appear.

Trying to time the stock market, most experienced participants agree, is a recipe for failure. Systematic in-and-out moves, or selling when all looks bleak, are documented paths to failure. Diversifying spreads risk and leads to an inner sense of calm.

When you have a lot of money in cash (banks, CDs, etc.), it doesn't earn a lot. I call it *successfully losing money safely*. Your money may have to last for twenty or thirty years. You cannot do that if your money is in cash. You actually are going backwards, or "losing money safely," because you are not keeping up with inflation. I will explain why I build inflation hedges into every portfolio decision.

Where We Are Headed

Joe the neighbor down the street may be quick to share his retirement experiences. His personal finances probably don't match yours and he is reluctant to share information about *them.* He most likely is not a retirement advisor and never has passed a license exam.

The government has many programs to help you get started toward saving (tax-deferred retirement accounts) or on a career course of your choice (student loans). Eventually, the government wants its money back. In "What you don't know about Social Security," I point out important dates to remember in dealing with the government and avoiding penalties. I tell the story of a woman who did not pay her required minimum distribution and incurred a 50 percent penalty as well as paying for the amount due. Moral: don't wait until the last minute to respond.

"Set It and Forget It" dashes the idea that dealing with a retirement plan ends the moment fun begins. Retirement plans are like physical and dental health. They need to be reviewed and adjusted with changes in your situation.

Finally, the financial industry has transformed rapidly. We will look to the future and suggest questions you may want to ask during the interview process, especially estate concerns.

In between, I'll share ways to connect with me for help, including my weekly radio shows, occasional webinars such as "Women Redefining Wealth" a recording of which is on my website, and short complementary consultations.

In the voyage from the 1980s, when I first was an advisor to today, the changes are profound. There are so many new products available. These include ETFs (exchange-traded funds that are modern improvements of mutual funds), fixed indexed funds (low-fee mutual funds or ETFs that trade lockstep with a market index), and discount brokerage firms.

Some investors choose ETFs and fixed indexed funds these days because their costs are lower. This is great if you know what you want to invest in and are constantly watching it. Most investors do not want to do that, however. Discount firms serve the same low-cost purpose although some traditional brokers have responded by dropping commissions altogether.

Most folks don't know how to diversify a portfolio and what allocations they should have. Finding out your risk tolerance, time frame, diversification needs, downside protection, tax questions, legacy planning and overall management are why people need personalized care through an established financial advisor.

Again, if you want to do it all yourself, that's great and you should. But the old adage applies here: *you get what you pay for*.

RETIREMENT AND THE TOGETHERNESS ADJUSTMENT

The most-asked questions I receive from clients are: "Can we afford to retire?" and "When?"

There are trickier questions to follow, ones that should be discussed by you and your spouse. Questions like "Will we be happy in retirement?" and "How are we going to spend our time?"

As your retirement advisor, we'll talk about your plans and goals in retirement and the financial implications such as how much money will be needed, what life expectancy may be. The money questions can be answered with some hard numbers. The soft-side questions of happiness and daily activities can be much tougher. They require considerable introspection on your part.

If physically possible, I insist that both partners be present for the interview process. They get to hear and gain an understanding of the financial plan. I get to hear their questions of me and whether both give answers to my questions that are in agreement.

I excel in addressing the numbers questions and build what is intended to be a worry-free plan. Will they be happy – that is pretty much up to them.

Sure, I can give generic pros and cons to topics such as relocating to a rural paradise or moving near the grandkids. Rural areas may be wonderful for hiking or water activities. If health conditions are an issue, however, how far away will medical facilities be? As grandchildren age, they will have lives and activities of their own that may not match the idyllic vision. If assisted care may be necessary soon, yes, moving close to the most responsible grown child may be the right answer.

Retirement is a major financial adjustment from saving to spending at a rate that your money will last. It is a major change from one or both partners going away to work each day to both being at home or traveling together all day. One wife, the same age and an engineer like her husband, insisted on a one-year head-start into retirement. She wanted to adjust to her new status before dealing with her husband's.

Before you retire from work, think about creating a social network in advance.

If your past identity was work, identify and start doing something you have always wanted to do. Learn a new skill, for instance. Create a bucket list, and do them!

If you are married and especially if you were a stay-at-home partner, now you have someone else in your space all day long. Get active and do it outside the home.

Some retirees decide to work part-time or turn a hobby into an entrepreneurial exercise. Others try volunteering or civic work. A career-long skill that may have turned into drudgery at the end can be used in a new way and become a fulfilling growth exercise.

At the end of the day, the apart time, work, or hobby can make for pleasant "How did your day go?" conversations.

I need a bigger nest egg

2

Cracking the Retirement Code

The stock market is complicated and mysterious enough without having to overlay all the aspects of retirement upon it.

Retirement is something most of us have never done before and it is a major shift both in lifestyle and in financial thinking. We are going from the accumulation phase of earning money and acquiring assets into a new income phase of living off our money. Our money has to last – well, we don't know how many years – and outliving our money is a nightmare we don't ever want to happen.

There are so many mistakes that can be made. Oh, my! How do we ever crack the retirement code?

How The Proprietary MAS Proprietary Process Can Guide You

Let's start with a history lesson. I started creating my proprietary MAS Proprietary Process back in the early 1980s, when I first became an advisor.

The M of my MAS Proprietary Process is for markets. I did a lot of stock and bond trading in those days. So, market is shorthand for the stock/bond markets.

The A of my MAS Proprietary Process is for alternatives. I have many clients who liked the types of investments that did not trade with the stock market. The *alternative* was then born. We called it limited partnerships in the ol' days.

So, I had two types of investments for clients: the stock/bond markets and limited partnerships.

The S of my MAS Proprietary Process is for safe money. As far as the *safe* investments go, we only had variable annuities available to us in the beginning of my career. The indexed or fixed annuities were just a distant thought at the time. The fixed annuities space wasn't born until about 1995. The fixed-indexed annuities started in the United States about twenty years ago.

So, this is a process we developed over many, many years. It was not officially called the MAS Proprietary Process until a year ago, but I have been using derivatives of it since 2012.

What Really Works Is Diversification

What would retirement be like without diversification?

Diversification is such a great tool to have for portfolios, and the MAS Proprietary Process is easy to understand. The MAS Proprietary Process really honed what works for clients, brings them peace of mind, and is easy to understand.

Diversification is such a great tool to have for portfolios, and the MAS Proprietary Process is easy to understand once they look at our MAS graph.

Take ten deep breaths.

Here is a plan that avoids the pitfalls. It cracks the retirement code, sweeping away the clutter and the mystery.

The concept is simplicity itself. Put 30 percent of your assets in each of three sectors and keep 10 percent in an emergency fund. Even if one sector is under pressure, the other two generally are doing comparatively well.

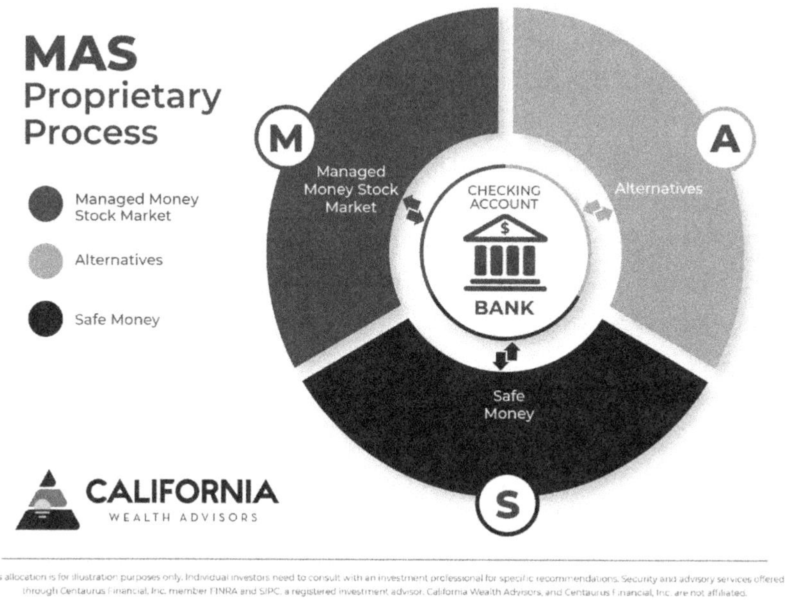

The proprietary process created by Kelley Slaught divides a portfolio into three portions of 30 percent each plus a 10% emergency reserve fund (not shown). The percentages would change depending on one's suitability/risk profile.

A Deeper Dive Into The MAS Proprietary Process

First, let's take a step back. For many of us, turning sixteen and learning how to drive a car is somewhat of a hazy memory.

Imagine if someone tried to give us a crash course in learning how to operate a car in just one week. Think of how hard it would be studying all the rules and regulations, getting in the car, and seeing which gadgets do what. This lever makes the seat go forward, that button adjusts the mirrors. Now how do I turn the windshield wipers on? You get the picture.

But wait, there is plenty more: parallel parking, setting the brake on a steep hill, defensive driving – what do you do if you see a ball rolling across the street? "We have practiced on an automatic transmission so let me introduce you to a stick shift," says your instructor. "You may be driving alone on a country road. You really need to know how to change a flat tire, use cables for a jump-start or fill the radiator – never with cold water! Look out, the road is icy. Which way do you turn?"

In the end, the all-in-one crash course would turn you into a nervous wreck. Maybe literally a crash and a wreck.

We'll take the MAS Proprietary Process at a more leisurely pace.

As mentioned, the plan breaks down into the three categories split 30 percent each plus an emergency reserve fund of about 10 percent.

The M (market) products are traded on exchanges. Stocks, mutual funds, exchange-traded funds, bonds are very liquid but can be quite volatile at times as the market goes up – or down.

The A (alternative components) are products that do not trade on the market. They generally are not as volatile. They are not as liquid, however, meaning they cannot be sold at a moment's notice.

The S (safe money) choices appeal especially to those clients who do not want to lose money. They want to preserve their capital. Some products have a floor, meaning you cannot lose your principal while you can participate in some of the growth to the upside. Examples of the relatively safe money include fixed-indexed annuities and products which can be constructed to have a floor and life insurance policies with long-term-care.

When I started in the industry in the early 1980s all three sectors existed but most of the alternative investments were limited partnerships. When I returned in 2012 after a break to raise my children, many more alternatives had cropped up. And new insurance products made me say wow.

With the advantage of perspective, I set out to delineate my MAS Proprietary Process.

Each of the sectors has appeal depending upon the client's risk tolerance, size of portfolio, and time horizon.

Many clients – at least when the market is rising – prefer the M (market) components for the volatility and the liquidity to quickly make portfolio changes.

Others like the A (alternative products) precisely because they are not liquid, they do not trade with the market. We inherently recognize that real estate, for example, is not liquid. The day you decide to buy a house you do not expect to sell it tomorrow.

Risk-adverse clients prefer the S (safe money) sector. They come to me, perhaps not aware of the choices. They tell me they do not want to lose any money. They want safety.

One place I usually help them invest in is annuity products or, life insurance with long-term-care coverage. They are guaranteed to never lose their principal. That gives many people peace of mind that they can't find in the M section with the market or the A section with alternative investments.

My job, of course, is to see that they put some money in each sector when appropriate.

I am big on diversification in portfolios. I like the diversification the MAS Proprietary Process brings with its three-way split and reserve fund for the unexpected. No matter what market we are in we are going to be making money or protecting our downside. It brings peace of mind to people that I couldn't provide them in the 1980s.

Even clients who are nervous about retirement or who are not financially savvy catch on before I can finish my explanation. They show signs of relief as their bodies relax. They realize they don't have to be all in the market in their investment portfolio. This is especially true of new clients making the jump from large brokerage firms or transferring their 401k/pensions to me.

Doing the right thing for the client often is more work than putting all their assets in one area. The ability to diversify is an advantage an independent broker brings. One size does not fit all and we strive to bring the best products we can find to our clients. The client always comes first.

I am pleased to make available to clients the entire spectrum of diversified portfolio options. Folks know that with my diversified MAS Proprietary Process that if the market is going up, they will participate in that. They know that if the market is going down, they have two investment classes expected to hold their value fairly well.

I am proud of my plan and the relief and comfort it brings to folks in retirement.

THE NUTS AND BOLTS OF FIXED-INDEXED ANNUITIES

Among the new possible retirement products available today are annuities. They are a type of insurance contract that can generate steady income in retirement. So, you can fund an annuity with either a lump sum or payments over time. They, like 401(k) accounts, are tax-deferred vehicles. So, you can buy annuities inside retirement accounts or outside retirement accounts.

There are several kinds of annuities and plenty of confusion. Writing in forbes.com, David Rodeck explains:

> A fixed index annuity provides steady payments that are based on the performance of an underlying index. Fixed index annuities offer some of the upside of investing in index funds, and may track the S&P 500, the Nasdaq, the Russell 2000 or the Hang Seng. Unlike index funds, fixed index annuities are generally protected against loss of principal. This means you won't lose any of the money you put into a fixed index annuity. This protection against losses, however, comes at a cost. You won't receive the exact return of the market index. Instead, the annuity will limit both your potential gains and your losses. This system makes an indexed annuity safer than investing directly in the market, though investing in a fixed annuity is more complicated than investing in an index fund.[3]

Sometimes people hear about bad experiences with some kinds of annuities. Most of the time, this is with variable annuities. If an annuity is right for you, it is a great vehicle to invest in. If it's not the right vehicle, then we'll do something else. So, I tend to take the time to explain what annuities are and what they do.

A fixed annuity is like a bond. An example: you put the money in for ten years for a rate of return of 2 percent. You get your money back after ten years, plus 2 percent, and you're done. That's a fixed annuity.

A variable annuity is on the other end of the spectrum. This is investing in the stock market. You're investing generally in mutual funds. So, it can go up with the market and guess what, it can go down with the market. You obviously can lose money in a variable annuity because it is invested in mutual funds. This is the type of annuity that generally gets a bad rap.

Another choice is a fixed-index annuity. What a fixed-indexed annuity does is track a particular index such as the S&P 500. You have the participation of the upside of the market. But if the market goes down, you have a floor. It's not going below that, so you have downside protection. People like that floor. Especially when they get into retirement, they want that protection. So, you can have growth with fixed index annuities, but you have that downside protection that you do not have with a variable annuity.

An example of a way to change a variable annuity to a fixed indexed annuity will be described here. I had a client come to me recently. She had about $800,000 in a variable annuity and it had appreciated a bit over these last couple of years, but not a lot due to a low performance and high fees. She was worried that a downturn could be coming. So, I suggested taking that variable annuity and putting it into a fixed-indexed annuity instead. A fixed-indexed annuity is a tax-favored accumulation product issued by an insurance company that is tied to a stock market index instead of an interest rate. This is called a 1035 Exchange. It's tax-free and very helpful for people.

She now has downside protection. She is no longer worried. She knows that it will appreciate with the market but has protection if the market turns down.[i][4]

A drawback of a fixed annuity, not tied to an index, is that these days they are not paying very much. So, I'm not having people do those. I'd rather do the fixed-indexed annuities for them. The fixed-indexed annuity is the best of both worlds, fixed or variable.

I have a whole team behind me that works to find the very best annuities for folks. They shop around to many different annuity companies. That is an advantage when you come to an independent financial advisor like me, you're not just getting one policy or provider. We work with about thirty different companies to find the best one, to get the lowest fees we can for you and the best results that we can find for you as well, be that income growth, LTC, or legacy planning.

If you have an annuity that is more than five years old, bring me your policy. Let's see if we can do better for you. Many times we can do a 1035 exchange. That is the process of transferring one insurance product – like yours – and replacing it with another in a "like kind" exchange. These exchanges are tax-free events. They work brilliantly for people who want to have downside protection.

PART II

Avoid These Six Biggest Retirement Blunders

"So much for counting on a lottery ticket to capitalize the retirement fund."

3

Not Having a Plan and Sticking to It

An adage often credited to Sir Winston Churchill is: "If you fail to plan, you are planning to fail."

Few would decide to take a lavishly expensive long vacation to Europe without having a plan.

Where would a football coach be without a game plan?

Embarking upon a twenty-year or thirty-year retirement without having a plan, and sticking to it, is unconscionable for many reasons.

Retirement is a journey that can last decades. The other trips we take pale in comparison.

Let's look at some trips we take that on rare occasions end in tragic headlines. Someone decides to go on a hike or wanders off from a campsite. Alone. If it is in a forest, they may get lost. Panic and confusion set it. Calls for help bring no answers. Instead of staying put, they invariably wander in circles. If it is mountainous country, they probably had started by going downhill. In their panic, they head uphill into more and more brush and tree-covered terrain, their clothes being caught and ripped.

Hiking alone in the stark beauty of the desert can be equally dangerous. The sun can be blisteringly hot. If the hiker started off without enough water and discovered poor cell reception, trouble can ensue.

Hikes alone in remote areas are not a good idea. If you fall and sprain an ankle or break a leg, who are you going to send for help?

Similarly, running out of gasoline or mechanical problems or a sudden blizzard on a side road may not have a pleasant ending.

Retirement is a long journey that can be ambushed by emotions and tight finances. Now you know why I and other advisors put so much emphasis on having a plan and sticking to it. Yes, plans can be adjusted as conditions change. Major causes for alterations such as a winning lottery ticket, a huge inheritance or selling real estate or a sudden and debilitating illness are uncommon.

Crafting A Plan You Can Stick To

Consultations with prospective clients are a way of getting acquainted and seeing if we have a good fit. I put a lot of time and energy into crafting customized retirement plans.

Some of the trip disasters mentioned previously are because individuals decided to travel alone. On this retirement journey, you are never alone. It is based on your expressions of needs and goals, and my years of experience in matching clients with the proper amounts of risk and diversity.

Stock markets can have stretches of emotional thrill rides at times. Like the lost hiker, one can lose sight of the goal. Having participated in the formation of the plan and thoroughly understanding it, however, helps you to stay on course.

Sticking to it is important. Markets tend to go up and down over the long haul. Those who panic and bail out of the rollercoaster car tend to do so at the very bottom and some may be afraid to get back on board for years.

I said this is not a journey you will take alone. My team and I are with you all the way. You become part of my family. I check on my clients regularly. When times look bleak is when you need my advice the most. The plans I craft have the MAS Proprietary Process as the foundation. Depending upon the individual, they will have 30 percent or so in market products for growth and liquidity, around 30 percent in alternative investments that are more stable but not as liquid, and another 30 percent in safe money instruments, some with guaranteed floors where you cannot lose your principal. Plus, you will have an emergency reserve fund for life's surprises.

I have a client who came to me a few years ago when he was retiring. He was transferring from another advisor. The client's portfolio and his risk tolerance were mismatched. We rolled his 401(k) to me into an IRA so we could diversify his assets and begin creating income streams for him in retirement.

His 401(k) could only offer him investments in the stock market and he was not comfortable with that. He needed income and some downside protection.

We ultimately created a nice portfolio for him that has growth, income, and downside protection.

He retired and we started sending him income every month. He had told us he needed a certain amount each month and we successfully started generating that for him. The income stream was not excessively deep but it was enough for him to live comfortably within the budget he had provided us.

About six months into his retirement, he decided he wanted to buy a very expensive car. He wanted to withdraw funds from his IRA to pay for it. He said it was too good a deal to pass up and he was really hooked. Unfortunately, I had to tell him that if he withdrew a large chunk of his principal, there would not be as much in the account to generate the income he needed, plus it is a fully taxable event. His monthly income would drop and he would have a harder time reaching his income needs. I recommended he not buy the car.

He decided he wanted to anyway and, of course, it was his money. We sent him the funds and ever since he has struggled to meet his income needs. I always encourage people to not withdraw the principal from their accounts, and only the income.

This was a case of not sticking to the plan. Eventually, that new car will not look nearly as pretty.

POOR PLANNING AND A RETIREMENT DREAM CRUSHED

This is a cautionary tale about someone we will call George (true story, but names and details changed to protect privacy). George was excited, his retirement dream was about to come true. He had been formulating it for years: Be nomads with his wife Ellen and spend about eighteen months or so making not one but two auto trips across the nation and back. Leisurely trips, taking them to whatever points of interest that called out to them.

The only problem was, George was nine years older than his wife. He retired at age sixty-five and played househusband and pursued hobbies of gardening and bicycling, waiting as patiently as he could for Ellen to reach age sixty-two and take early retirement.

George had a friend who had done a similar nomadic experience and thus he had a sort of template to follow. A few months before Ellen's retirement date, something nagged at George, however. The trip would be in their SUV to major stopping points or base camps. By day they would bicycle to state parks, museums, and to caves – Ellen's favorite.

George was in fine physical condition, riding for an hour and a half each day. But if something came up to delay the trip for a couple years, say, would a sudden illness cause the dream to go unrealized? Ellen had a full-time desk job. Would she be up to rigorous exercise each day? Further, there would be a ton of details to tend to that could not be accomplished until Ellen quit the working world.

The couple had been married for about forty years. They had three grown children living in scattered points on the West Coast, and Ellen's extended family living in small towns on the East Coast. Their son was a bachelor, both daughters were married with jobs outside the house. One daughter had an elementary-school-age girl and a heavier parenting load when her pilot husband was away. The other daughter was married with two pre-school boys eighteen months apart and a frazzling career loaded with responsibilities.

Their life in the Red Zone as full retirement approached pretty much had a fixed routine. Ellen was the breadwinner during the week. On probably half the weekends she would spend Saturdays baking, canning produce, fixing meals for the week ahead, and sewing, a favorite hobby. Househusband George would spend Saturdays doing life's errands, physical conditioning or watching sports programming. Sundays were for relaxing, church, and potluck dinners with friends.

Half the weekends their routine was interrupted. Their daughter with two very small, energetic boys was overwhelmed. Ellen would commute to a city about four hours away by car or an hour-plus flight to babysit, do laundry or grocery shop. She really enjoyed that and felt needed.

George would go mentally through the preparations for the grand trip. There was the fun part, gathering information on possible sights to see and prioritizing list after list. There was the financial part, disposing of back-home responsibilities, and financing eighteen months of travel.

The couple – and the bank – owned four houses, but none was free and clear and they still had student loan debt from their kids' college days. For the trip of a lifetime, George would sell the primary house they were living in and one rental, using proceeds to finance the trip. One rental would become their new primary residence upon their return and the remaining rental would be sold then.

They wouldn't need two cars on the trip, so one would be sold. Everything they were taking had to fit in a SUV, so furniture had to be put in storage for the duration. Could their primary residence be sold just before they were to leave on their trip? What if it could not be sold in time?

There were hints of the challenges ahead. The furnishings, it turned out, filled not one but three large storage places. Worried about whether their primary house would sell quickly in the early spring prime selling season, George tested the waters the previous fall. The house sold quickly – too quickly – and October was a blur of open houses and four days' notice of a speed-up in the escrow close. They sold their second car but just days later their SUV was totaled by a young driver. No injuries thankfully, but their lives were filled with the unexpected. Find an interim rental car, make an insurance claim, get a car loan, find extended-stay lodging for a couple months until the start of the trip.

Ellen was unhappy about abandoning her grandmother role. She insisted, and George finally agreed, that every four or six weeks no matter where they were, she could fly to the grandkids' for a mini-vacation.

They had a plan and they embarked on the trip of a lifetime in January 2020. Six weeks later, COVID hit.

As you can imagine, the trip had to be scrapped. The couple was now homeless. George inquired about moving into their future primary home sixteen months early. The people living in it had an iron-clad contract for a two-year lease. No deal.

George was overwhelmed – no place to live in, unexpected costs, a skimpy reserve fund, a dream dashed and uncertainty at every turn. He became more and more reserved. For couples, retirement can be a long adjustment process. Their marriage was now under strain.

No one could see the onset of COVID. Yet, this was a planning process that went awry. Could some of the mistakes have been avoided?

Admittedly, with the advantage of hindsight, I believe so. Let's count the mistakes.

- The couple never met with a retirement coach or a financial planner. They went it alone.
- The questionnaire I give prospective clients asks about their finances, their risk tolerance and their retirement goals. The interview process would have shown that student debt in retirement is a red flag. The couple was not risk-tolerant either in finances or their lifestyle.

- Retirement is a major adjustment and it can take months or a year to decompress from the work world and adjust to plenty of leisure time. The younger wife really had no chance to relax before being immersed in preparations for a national tour doubled.
- One partner had the travel bug, the other was a homebody. The written questionnaire and my follow-up interviews likely would have shown that they had different interests and expectations from retirement.
- The housing market where they lived was red hot. Landlord George surely knew that although few would have guessed how hot. Home is security, especially for a homebody. Being homeless upon entering retirement had to drive someone of that temperament up the wall.
- One option the couple had was to hire a property manager and rent out their primary house for their trip. The rent would have covered their costs, the property manager would have handled all details, and the property would have continued to appreciate in value. That conversation never happened as they never talked to a professional.
- Another option would have been to do a 1031 real estate exchange, deferring any tax gain on their house.
- As it turned out the house they sold in the $300s gained $100,000 in value by twelve months later. Of course, I would have told them the student debt should have been paid off long ago and their reserve fund was not nearly enough. Paying it off now was a good idea even if long overdue. Coincidentally, that debt was $100,000.

4

Making Decisions Emotionally

Entire books have been written about the psychology of investing and emotions overcoming logic in making financial decisions.[5] Investors can get way too exuberant when market indexes set new records seemingly almost week after week.[6] Conversely, when the market plunges day after day, the tendency is to panic.[7]

Younger investors have time to recover from their mistakes. Retirees or those about to, do not have that luxury. If they get too exuberant and become too aggressive, a correction can raise fears that their principal may run out. If they bail out during white knuckle time, they may sell at the very bottom and be afraid to get back in.

When emotions take over, the effects on the portfolio are not pretty. There are many steps to building a portfolio that can weather the seasons, good and bad. Let's assume that you start your retirement voyage with a well-crafted plan. Yet if emotions take control of the throttle, watch out. The results can be devastating.

Retirement is supposed to be stress-free, a time to do what you want. If financial deadly sins pop up, however, retirement can be anything but stress-free.

As an advisor I spend considerable time matching client risk tolerance with the risk they take on. That tends to bring peace of mind instead of panic.

Financial Deadly Sins Can Harm Your Portfolio

In classic literature the seven deadly sins, also known as the cardinal sins, are a grouping and classification of vices within Christian teachings, although they are not specifically mentioned in the Bible. According to the standard list, they are: pride, greed, wrath, envy, lust, gluttony, and sloth.

Here are some of my deadly financial sins to avoid:

Pride is one of the deadly financial sins. Thinking that you can beat the market by picking individual stocks or selecting actively managed funds or timing the market is not a plan. When it does not work out, you have to deal with crushed pride. Day traders revel in what they are earning during a great year. You do not hear so much in the down years. I actually had a day trader admit how his trading turned sour and he went negative.

You need to make sure that pride does not get in the way of your portfolio. The antidote to that is humility. Accepting average rates of return can be very good. That gives you peace of mind. I usually look somewhere between 4 percent and 9 percent as an average rate of return I'm seeking for most folks.

Greed is not good financially. Greed is something you can probably afford to have more of earlier in your life, but it's dangerous to be greedy in retirement.

Being greedy, wanting to have more and more money, more aggressive returns, is not a good plan. The antidote to that of course is moderation. Make sure that you maintain your rebalancing of your portfolio.

I did a portfolio review for a client and I did recommend that she purchase a popular car stock. Two years later, she's eighteen times above what she invested in it. Oh, boy was that a good recommendation. Here is what we'll do, I told her. We will sell half and take out the initial investment. So, then we're playing with house money, as they say at the casino. But here is the difference. We are taking our profits off that. If you want to take some of your money and be risky with it, you can. But don't get greedy and see your profits vanish.

Envy is another deadly sin. I talk people off the ledges from envy. So "Joe" down the street told them to buy this, that and the other. And it's always funny because Joe down the street is probably not a financial advisor. Does he really know when to buy something or when to sell something? So let's not be envious of our neighbors. Make sure you are not envying some guy down the street and that you are doing what is actually best for you.

Gluttony is sinful as well. That is when you are failing to save. You must have that conversation with yourself that you are living beyond your means. You can't invest what you haven't saved. Starting to save today is never a bad idea. A good antidote, many of my clients find, is to automatically have money transferred from their checking account into their account with us each month. This builds financial wealth.

Aggressive taking on of risk is a deadly financial sin. You may be making a load of money in the good years but in the bad years you're probably losing a lot of money. That can lead to nervousness, to worry, to panic.

Impatience should be on the deadly sin list. Well, I guess 2008 was a good lesson in having patience, wasn't it?

A lot of people bailed out of the markets that year. A new client told me recently she has been in cash since late 2008. Well, she's missed out on the biggest bull market we've seen in years and years. You must have some patience with financial markets. You really do. If you bailed on the United States market in 2008, you missed out on an average return of about 16 percent a year.

The antidote is to have some patience and some knowledge of financial history. History does repeat itself. Many times, sharp declines are followed by strong rebounds.

Consider what happened in 2020. When the pandemic hit in 2020, I had many clients in the market in March, April, and May when prices went down so much. I did not have anyone panic. I did not sell out of anything. We stayed the course. We had a plan, we had diversification.

We didn't know at the time that the market would come back quickly. So, avoid these financial sins.

Is Timidness A Deadly Sin?

I did not but sloth on my financial deadly sins list, but of course laziness is not good. Perhaps I should add timidness to the list. I will never forget the time I met a timid investor we will call Carla (true story, but names and details changed to protect privacy).

Carla was an extremely shy prospect who came in a few years ago. She was good friends with a long-time client of mine. My client had been working with me for years and was very comfortable with me, my firm, and the integrity I bring to my business. She loved the way I took care of my clients and had their best interests at heart – always. My client enjoyed the diversification in her accounts and the downside protection in a portion of her portfolio.

When her shy friend Carla worked up the courage to come in and see me, I could tell she was hesitant. I went over what she had, her risk tolerance, time horizon, and the rest. We came up with a great plan to alter her current portfolio so it was more in line with her specific goals.

When we had finished the process, she said I made it so easy to understand. She said she felt very comfortable because I never tried to sell her anything. I simply explained what she had and how it could be improved. She knew I could be trusted because her friend spoke so highly of me.

Once she finally decided to come in for a consultation, Carla told me she wished she had come in to see me years before.

I actually hear that a lot. Many people tell me that no one ever explained investing to them or what is available to them in such a clear manner.

Don't let timidness keep you from exploring an opportunity.

QUESTIONS, WE GET LOTS AND LOTS OF QUESTIONS

As owner and principal of California Wealth Advisors, I believe in educating clients. I take my job seriously. Many clients are entering a process they have never done before. If they are not in the financial field, the terms and some of the concepts may seem like Greek to them.

There are several ways to reach me or to access the information I provide in different forums. Let's take them one by one:

My name is spelled Kelley (with two e's) and Slaught. The website is https://www.californiawealthadvisors.com/.

I can be reached at Kelley@californiawealthadvisors.com

There are past and present webinars you can view. They tend to focus on a particular topic with plenty of tips. Look on the website https://www.californiawealthadvisors.com/

I offer no-cost obligation consultations to persons with a sufficient amount of investable assets, $200,000 or more of investable assets if you're serious about your portfolio. Our MAS plan works better for 1mm or more, but we generally never turn anyone away that we feel we can work with.

There is also a weekly radio show you can listen to, either live or view archived transcripts. The show is on KRLA, 870 am live from 3 to 4 p.m. (PT) Saturdays in Southern California. If you are out of signal reach, you can listen live on the station's website https://www.am870theanswer.com/radioshow. Or use the archives: scroll down to the S's for "Kelley's Bull Market News" and my photo.

Another resource of course is this book in your hand. You may want to keep your copy for possible future review while acquiring another copy for a friend.

The questions tend to be the same regardless of the forum. Still, they are quite fresh, especially if it is your question too and you have not found the answer.

Some of the most asked questions are:

How do I diversify my assets?

I don't want to be 100 percent in the stock market, how can I do something different?

Can I retire? And when?

I don't like risk, what can I do to protect my assets?

I want to leave my assets to my heirs. How do I do that?

Can I get some long-term-care coverage with modern life insurance policies?

My advisor never calls me. How do you keep up with your clients?

The Q&A sessions are fun for me and the audience. Let's try a few.

Santa Barbara: Do you see inflation going up and perhaps even faster?

Kelley: It just has to but it's not a bad thing, actually. When inflation increases, that means people are making more money on their savings accounts and different types of investments. I just don't want it to go up fast. The same with interest rates. I want interest rates to rise slowly. That is when we have big runs in the market.

Burbank: Is it too late to turn it around?

My husband and I are raising our grandchildren. Their parents passed away years ago. We were both retired back then. Although I've since gone back to work part-time, we're now in our mid-seventies with two teenagers who will want to go to college in the next few years. Our retirement plan obviously never considered this as a possibility.

Kelley: I always tell people it's never too late to turn anything around. I did have this same situation with a client a few years ago. It was heartbreaking because they were in retirement, and they really had slowed down. All of a sudden, they had to raise a couple of kids and God bless them for that. They had some hard choices to make. There just was not a lot of dollars to go around. They had to cut back on expenses as much as they could. Given the circumstances, perhaps a community college would work best for your grandkids the first two years.

Los Angeles: When the unexpected happens, can retirement plans be altered?

Oh yes. We alter plans all the time. People inherit money. They sell real estate and all of a sudden, they have a big chunk of cash in the bank and what do with it? I make sure to keep in touch with my clients and ask if anything changed for them.

About thirty years ago my aunt and uncle won the Arizona lottery. Huge as in $20 million worth. So that was a life-changer for them. They did move into a more expensive house in a golf community. It was a little awkward because their friends were in retirement at that point. They had a hard time making friends in the new community. Eventually, they moved back into their former community.

Santa Ana: My mother wants to give me her IRA. How can that work?

Mother is in an assisted living community and she asked me to watch it for her. I have been keeping up on her required minimum distributions and she told me that she just wants me to have it.

Kelley: She cannot give you her IRA. She could sell everything that's in the IRA and take out cash and give that to you as the daughter. However, that is a taxable event to her at her ordinary tax rate. I would need more details about her tax bracket and the size of the IRA. Probably it is best for your daughter to wait until she passes away and inherit a beneficiary IRA. There are other options that could be explored in a consultation.

Huntington Beach: My mom is seventy-nine and she has no tolerance for risk with her nest egg. Is an annuity a good idea?

Mom has more income than she will ever need because of my dad's military pension that she is receiving now. I'm considering an annuity for that because she does not need the income and it is a way to protect the principal.

Kelley: I would say yes. Annuities can serve great purposes. If this is an annuity outside of a retirement account, your mom puts the money in there. Then you'll inherit that money tax free. Let's say she puts in $100,000 and she passes away five years later. It might be worth $150,000 then and the $50,000 is taxable to you. But the $100,000 is not. So that's a great way for asset passing.

I have an extremely high net worth client that wants his children to inherit his assets as tax-free as he can. So, he and his wife are buying large annuities each year. The annuities grow, tax-deferred, and are there if they ever need it, but will go to their children upon death on a mostly tax-free basis. It's a great way to transfer wealth.

"Great plan. Could we get some more details?"

5

Trying to Time the Stock Market

In or out, or at the bottom, trying to time the stock market is a losing strategy. Avoid the blunder of trying to time the market.

About once a decade the stock market is rattled by what headline writers call a "crash" or what financial analysts and scholars label a "correction," meaning a drop of 20 percent or more in the S&P 500 Index.

Well-known journalist Jayne Bryant Quinn in a retrospective piece three months after the March 2020 COVID Crash rattled off six downturns in the half century before 2020.[8] Among them:

- Market plunge of 1973-74 (stocks down 48 percent)
- Black Monday, Oct. 19, 1987 (down 22.6 percent in one day)
- 2000 Tech-Stock Crash (stocks sliced in half)

- Real estate crash of 2006 (stocks down by half from 2007 to 2009)
- March 2020 Covid crash (followed by a quick recovery)

Her conclusion: "It's never the end of the world. Stock and bond index funds, plus patience, always win."

These "corrections" or "crashes" purge the market of excesses, puncture the "This time it is different" thinking, and cause the phones of wealth advisors to light up. Some unfortunate souls reject professional advice and inevitably bail out at the very bottom. Worse, they are too scared to re-enter the market and they miss huge bull runs. The motto for my weekly radio show is "There's always something to be bullish about" and that decidedly positive outlook is borne out time and again by the recoveries that follow as memories of the headlines fade.

Many people bailed out in 2008, failed to come back in, and a decade later had missed one of history's great bull market runs.

I also tell the experiences of my clients who did not panic, who did not bail out during the Covid Crash of March 2020. The reasons may surprise you. It is not just what I – and they – did then but the education and preparations we did before.

The question during the rollercoaster dives is "Should I bail out?" Bailing out is an emotionally driven question better phrased as "Should I try to time the market now?" Whether we are addressing the question of a panic bailout or an intentional strategy of repeatedly entering and exiting the market, the answer is the same: Timing the market does not work. It is an almost universal opinion of professionals everywhere. I will include a few samples of how they put it in their own words.

I do help clients with all kinds of financial matters, but retirement planning is the bulk of how I spend my days and weeks. Clients in the Red Zone, close in time to the retirement decision, are aware that this is not when they should intentionally put their life savings at risk. You won't find day traders among clients seeking my advice or, I dare say, among those of reputable advisors elsewhere. The reason? The initial consultations and information sharing are an exercise in matchmaking between advisor and prospective client. Do we have a good fit? Advisors want to help people, not enable them in risky practices that may head them toward poverty in their later years.

Education and preparation are key to staying calm during economic shocks.

At California Wealth Advisors, here's how that works. In our meet and greet chats, the answers to the printed questionnaire and the examination of personal records of assets and debts, is how we gain a picture of you and your financial situation. We ask probing questions about your risk tolerance. Many pre-retirees do not have any idea of what it really is. They may not know just what kind of companies their mutual funds own shares in. Maybe the risk involved was appropriate for their much younger self, but not as retirement approaches.

Education is something I believe in and the hours I invest in informing clients pay off later in times of anxiety. I stress the three-pronged plus emergency reserve of the MAS Proprietary Process. You are splitting your portfolio three ways, I tell clients. If one sector is under stress, the other two should be doing comparatively well. The pep talk becomes apparent during an inevitable correction. Clients actually see that their portfolio is not getting walloped as much as some benchmark index.

Although it should be obvious, there is a secret to stock market indexed funds we do not see. They are designed to track the index efficiently at minimal cost. Track the index they follow. When the market goes up, the fund goes up. When the market goes down, the fund does too with the indexes. If your work 401(k) is in index funds, you get low fees but a lockstep performance. If the index (stock market) goes down, your index's goal is to match that index. Probably not going to yield you a good return, but your fees will be low. Is that good enough for you? Industry studies estimate that professional financial advice could add to a portfolio's return over time compared to a client's portfolio not receiving any professional financial advice.[9]

Your relationship with a professional, however, does not ban human adjustments. The beauty of the MAS approach is that if one sector is not doing well at the moment, some portion can be transferred to the other two. This is done sparingly, and in a defensive manner. It is not a time-the-market approach.

Aside from moments of panic, we doubt that people of retirement age advised by reputable professionals are into market-timing approaches. We promised a sampling of why experienced professionals do not believe in market timing. Here goes:

- Alan Roth of AARP in "10 Years After the Drop, More Proof You Can't Time the Market"[10]: On March 9, 2019 the stock market marked a tenth birthday of a strong bull run. That is a 411 percent return or 17.7 percent annually from that bleak time in 2009. The real estate crash of 2006, to be sure, had taken its toll. As measured by a low-cost index fund, the market had dropped 55 percent over the prior seventeen months.

  Let's measure the performance from the seventeen months prior when the market peaked. A $10,000 investment on Oct. 9, 2007 would be worth $22,760 on the tenth birthday, still a respectable 7.5 percent return.

- A wealth manager, Mark Fonville, now in Richmond, VA[11]: "I learned many experiences from that [2008] experience. Two of those are: 1) Don't time the stock market. 2) Stick with your investment plan."

- Jim Wong of Forbes:[12] "Timing your trades makes you an active investor seeking to outperform the market. You have to predict who the winning companies or sectors are going to be each year. You must choose the right stocks at the right price and at the right time… A 2019 Vanguard study indicates that only 35 percent of active fund managers beat their market benchmark."

- Pippa Stevens and CNBC.com compiled a chart from Bank of America data of market performance by decades.[13] It showed:

Decade	Price Return
1930	-42 percent
1940	35 percent
1950	257 percent
1960	54 percent
1970	17 percent
1980	227 percent
1990	316 percent
2000	-24 percent
2010	190 percent
2020	18 percent

  Since 1930 the gain has been 17,715 percent.
  Note that the market went up in eight of the ten of the decades.

- Maurie Backman of The Motley Fool Investing:[14] "Dollar-cost averaging (investing a specific dollar amount at regular intervals) takes emotions and fear out of the equation."

- Fisherinvestments.com:[15] "For a long-term investor, we believe it is prudent to be in the market unless you have strong reasons – unclouded by emotion and bias – to believe a bear market is under way. Bear markets, where the market is down 20 percent or more, generally come on slowly and rarely announce themselves."

LOWER YOUR RISK: DIVERSIFY

Don't put all your eggs in one basket, conventional wisdom advises. Once in a while, a witty contrarian has a tongue-in-cheek counter, "Put all your eggs in one basket – and then guard it very carefully."

Diversify, diversify, diversify, I say. The conventional wisdom is right – although I will come back to that witty contrarian later, acknowledging that extreme diversification may not be prudent either.

Diversifying is an investment strategy to lower risk by spreading your holdings among various asset classes and sectors that differ in reacting to outside forces such as the particular stage of the economic cycle or a shock to the system – a virus that kills 600,000 Americans or the terrorist attack of 9/11.

The strategy lowers risk but it is not intended to increase your rate of return. An investor who selects a handful of companies that react the same way to a market trend may handily outperform a more diversified investor or a benchmark over the short term. Over the long run, however, that star performance comes back to earth. You may double the return of the S&P 500 in a given month but can you do it over three years? Your retirement portfolio is a marathon, not a sprint. Your money may have to last for twenty or thirty years. [16]

In spreading your risk, you want asset classes or companies that perform differently in any stage of the economic cycle. One selection may be soaring, but a couple of others may be in a deep funk. You have lowered your risk but lessened your possible rate of return. In the early days of the automobile, inventors found that four pistons made for a smoother ride than two. To a point. You don't see many cars with thirty-two pistons today.

There are many ways to diversify.

Starting with my MAS Proprietary Process, clients automatically get a healthy dose of diversification. Their assets, based on their comfort level toward risk, are put in three sectors. Choices in each sector can increase with the size of the portfolio.

Cash. Retirees may come to our firm with a boatload of cash. They may have taken a lump payment on a company pension – a decision best discussed with us first. They may have had to cash out some company stock options. Or they may have sold real estate to finance travel or cut ties when they are away. Too much cash, however, is a failure to diversify and may not provide a good rate of return. There is a need to invest your excess cash into other assets. When you leave money in cash, we call it "successfully losing money safely." This is because you are not keeping up with inflation and your dollar today *does not* equal a dollar tomorrow.

Timing. There is a danger called sequence of returns. Meaning, if you invest all at once, you are vulnerable to a sudden drop the next day. It is better to invest that cash-rich portfolio in stages.

Company risk. Buying two automobile manufacturers spreads the risk that a given company may falter in a major way. Buying six auto companies or six firms associated in the industry – parts suppliers, assembly companies, dealerships, accessory sellers – does not spread risk. If the economy goes into a recession, automobile purchases can be delayed and all the companies may suffer.

Large companies or small. Small-capitalization companies tend to outperform their behemoth rivals over the long haul. Large companies, however, may have the cash and the borrowing power to survive a recession. Owning a mix of large and small is a way to diversify.

Company life-stage. Companies echo humans in a way. New ones are like teenagers, growing rapidly and eating everything in the refrigerator or all the cash they can borrow to fuel growth. The growth companies often are not profitable – at least yet – and may be judged by how much of a market niche they are rapidly acquiring. Mature companies, say a maker of soups or canned vegetables, are stable, probably pay dividends to keep investors interested, but may have to focus more on increasing the efficiency of production lines than in seeking new markets.

Mutual funds. A general mutual fund is a way to diversify. It may own stock in 200 or more companies and debt in many others. Buying a sector mutual fund is a way to add emphasis in a particular sector, say health care or technology. The S&P 500 classifies companies by eleven sectors: Communication Services, Consumer Discretionary, Consumer Staples, Energy, Financials, Health Care, Industrials, Materials, Real Estate (recently granted its own status) Technology and Utilities. Owning two general mutual funds may not be a good idea because of duplication in holdings. Similarly, a family of mutual funds may offer ones with different names such as growth, value, dividend payers and more. Take a close look, however, and a star performer in one of the family funds can be found in several more. Look how many times Apple may appear. Stock intersection is what we see very often in families of funds – even with different names.

Overdiversification. Let's return to our witty, tongue-in-cheek contrarian investor. It is possible to overdiversify. Individual investors managing their own accounts and a primary job to boot, may be pressed to keep up if they own more than six to twelve companies. Feel free to ask your investment advisor about his or her strategy in diversifying versus over diversifying.

"When I retire I hope for a soft landing."

6

Failing to Properly Diversify

Among my favorite sayings is: "Successfully losing money safely." This term refers to the damage inflation can do to a retirement portfolio, sneaking up subtly and causing significant harm before an investor realizes it. Either a portfolio beats the rate of inflation, or it falls behind, leaving the investor worse off than where she or he started.

Actually, that is only the half of the story. You have heard the expression "*idle* cash." If a risk-averse investor sells an asset and puts it in cash for a period of time, the damage by inflation can be measured in two ways. First, the real rate of return on that money is a negative number: zero earnings minus the rate of inflation compounded over the time period. Second, there is an opportunity cost. If invested prudently, the cash might have beaten the rate of inflation resulting in a positive number.

Much is misunderstood about inflation – how it is measured, whether it can be predicted accurately, whether indexes include or do not include food and energy. Let's clear up some of that confusion with an example.

Hedge Your Portfolio For Loss Of Purchasing Power

I had a client, let's call her Ruth, who came to me recently with about $1 million in her IRA. Ruth had the funds fully invested in 2008 but lost $500,000 of her portfolio in that financial downturn. She panicked, liquidated all her assets to cash, and remained in cash until she recently met me.

Since Ruth was only earning a nominal rate in the money market account in her IRA for all those years, she essentially lost 2 percent to 3 percent a year because of inflation over that time frame. She was "successfully losing money safely." Her funds were in cash and therefore were not fluctuating with the market. That gave her peace of mind. But at what cost?

Her $1 million in 2008 was really worth $1.2 million in today's dollars. This is what inflation will do to your portfolio. You will lose money – buying power – on those funds when you are in cash.

Also, since she was in cash for so many years and we have seen one of the biggest bull market runs in history over the last ten to twelve years, she really missed out.

If she had invested her funds, yes with the ups and downs that go along with that and had received a 7 percent return on her money over those years, her $1 million would be worth more than $2 million today.

So, with her and with so many others who fear the market and become stagnant, we utilized the S for safe part of my MAS Proprietary Process so that her funds would be in the safe, downside protected investment pool. Ruth is now extremely happy that she met me and knows she is no longer losing money safely.

The three-pronged MAS Proprietary Process has an A for Alternatives section, especially real estate, that has inherent inflation hedges built in. Some clients buy investment properties with tenants agreeing to automatic rent increases each year of about 2 percent. Since the increases are automatic, the investor retirees have real peace of mind. They know that inflation will not be controlling them, but that they have a handle on the insidious portfolio robber.

We sense inflation's toll even if we don't have a calculator. Search back in your memory twenty or thirty years for the price of a given item. A big-ticket purchase such as a house or a car. Or consider a frequent purchase such as a regular house cleaning, haircut, or the commodity we love to gripe about, a gallon of gasoline. Twenty or thirty years is how long your retirement may last and a guide to lost purchasing power in the future.

For those saving for a far-away retirement date, growth vehicles are a way to compensate. The total value of your account is likely to grow even as inflation nibbles away at the purchasing power of each dollar. Receiving the last paycheck, however, changes the equation. You no longer work so your money must now work for you.

A portfolio loading with fixed-interest rate vehicles – bonds or savings accounts, for example – may do OK in year one but fast forward to year eight or ten. It is getting quite a bit harder to pay the bills without touching the principal. Lifestyle adjustments, cutting the little luxuries, already have been made. How to bring in more interest income without taking on more risk becomes one question. Can a change in assets bridge the gap?

If someone holds a large amount of long-term bonds, a rise in interest rates creates a cruel paradox. The bonds you own are paying less than the new bonds being issued. The face value of *your* bonds will drop accordingly to rise up to the new norm in bond yields.

The popularity of asset classes has changed in today's environment. Interest rates are at historically low levels. Bonds and certificates of deposit are being recommended less and less.

Inflation's sneak attack on purchasing power especially hits do-it-yourself portfolios. Those who choose to forego professional help may not be as up to date on the inverse relationship of interest rates and inflation. When interest rates rise, inflation tends to decline.[17] They may not be as aware of new investment alternatives.

Americans approaching retirement age tend to remember the late 1970s and early 1980s when sharp inflation raged out of control before being calmed by astronomically high interest rates.

My concern is not hyper-inflation – we'll deal with it when and if it gets closer. Rather, I concentrate on beating today's 2 percent to 3 percent inflation with hedges built into my client recommendations. This can be done in a couple of ways. One, the entire portfolio can be nudged slightly toward the growth end of the spectrum. Two, I look at the ability of particular asset choices to rise if prices in general go up. Not all companies or consumers are affected equally; producers of commodities such as lumber or copper may do well even as heavy buyers of the products suffer.18

Inflation's effects and how we measure them can be confusing. One concept is that those who borrow money at today's prices and pay it back years later with reduced purchasing power may actually benefit. Think homeowners or holders of stocks in what is called asset inflation. Of course, retirement is not the greatest time to be in debt. It is also not the time to be in debt if the interest rate is variable. This would be a good time to consider locking a variable-rate mortgage into a fixed-rate mortgage.

There are several ways to measure the rate of inflation. The Bureau of Labor Statistics measures the prices of 80,000 consumer prices to create an index. It collects price information from thousands of retail and service companies frequented by a sample of 14,500 families. What is called the core rate of the Consumer Price Index excludes food and energy prices which are volatile. Of course, we all eat and use fuel to travel or heat our homes. Another version includes those.19

In most years, Social Security recipients get an automatic cost-of-living adjustment (COLA), usually announced in October. It wasn't always so. It took a separate act of Congress each year until the large price increases of the mid-1970s forced a change.

The Social Security Administration publishes a chart of the annual increases from 1975 to the present.[20] It can be found at https://www.ssa.gov/oact/cola/colaseries.html.

The COLA increases this century have been relatively modest. In 1980 the increase was 14.3 percent; in 1981 it was 11.2 percent.

In 2021 the Federal Reserve indicated it would maintain a target rate of 2 percent inflation but with upward adjustments, if necessary, to prop up the economy.

Historically, economists have had difficulty predicting inflation with any degree of accuracy. That is why I use the current rate as a planning assumption until strong evidence suggests otherwise.

In any event, if someone offers you a penny for your thoughts, negotiate. What does a single penny buy anymore?

LIFE'S CHALLENGES GENERATE QUESTIONS

We get questions, often about common life situations that occur during retirement. Personal challenges are often easier to resolve with an experienced advisor assisting.

What are the implications of divorce in retirement?

The personal and financial impacts of divorce can be overwhelming, especially when trying to adjust to retirement. Real estate, retirement savings, pensions, stock options or even a family business need to be divided equitably. All this while keeping in mind life insurance proceeds, long-term care insurance policies and debt pay-down. In simpler estates, where the parting is not acrimonious and the best way to divide assets is obvious, a new form of divorce law – agreed divorce – is evolving. One attorney draws up the documents. Near the end, a second attorney gets involved to review and protect the interests of one of the spouses. Litigation costs can be reduced dramatically.

Can I leave more money to one child than another?

Yes, and without proper estate planning many people do it without being aware. While an even split among heirs is the most common, there are situations where an uneven split may be necessary, especially in the case of blended families or when special needs children are in the picture.

How do I say no to my adult children's request for money?

Saying no to an adult child who is hurting or in need can be difficult and it is possible you set yourself up for this through your previous actions. The real world is full of disappointments and neither you, your spouse nor your adult child can afford to delay the inevitable. Always make sure you have enough to live before giving money to loved ones.

Do I need to save money in retirement?

Yes. People should still find ways to save money during retirement, particularly during the early years.

Is working part-time a good idea in retirement?

For new retirees, the idea of part-time employment to fill financial gaps and maintain social connections is gaining popularity.

Should couples stagger their retirement dates?

The question is sometimes called 'in-synch" or "out-of-synch" retirement. The answer is... it depends. One of the working spouses may want a head-start to organize the household and develop outside interests. Other couples may wish to plunge right in to major trips – together.

I have lost my spouse. What are some of the decisions I need to be aware of?

Most experts say to take time, possibly a year for emotions to settle down, before making major decisions. Among financial implications you should be aware of:

What about tax-filing status?

It will change and possibly could move you into a higher bracket. You can file married filing jointly the year your spouse dies. Then you file as a single person or in some cases as head of household.

What about a Social Security cut?

There will be one Social Security check instead of two, generally the amount the higher-earning spouse received. Social Security also pays a one-time death benefit.

Any concerns with tax-deferred accounts?

Many people look to make up for lost income with retirement account withdrawals. Be aware of age restrictions and that taxes must be paid on the withdrawals at ordinary income rates. Some surviving spouses transfer the retirement account assets into their own name, which allows further postponing taxation.

Can over-focusing on kids be a problem?

Women in particular fall prey to this problem. They start worrying about the kids' inheritance and well-being even though they have been dealt a difficult situation and should put their needs first.[xviii][21]

“What do you see in emerging markets?”

7

Taking Advice from the Wrong Sources

Who can we turn to in preparing for retirement? This reminds me of the tale about my client, who we shall call Gregory. He and I had been chatting on the phone. Gregory was a white-collar executive, pushing sixty, and had so many questions about retirement that he decided to reach out to me. We had pretty well finished – over the phone – what could have been an initial consultation.

His next step, I explained, was to schedule an appointment, bring in the financial records I needed, and to fill out a questionnaire.

Next, I would prepare a retirement plan based upon his needs, goals, risk tolerance and such. Would he like to do so?

"You threw a lot at me," Gregory responded. "I want to think it over and to run it by my girlfriend first."

"Oh," I asked innocently, "what does she do?"

"She is on welfare," Gregory replied.

An executive who had around $500,000 in the bank was turning to someone on welfare for retirement financial advice.

Stunned, I choked back saying what I was thinking and invited him to get back to me when he was ready.

The Mystery Is Real

Retirement is a complex process most of us have never gone through before. We don't know what to expect, we don't know if our savings measure up to reality, we aren't even sure if we will soon get bored with too much free time.

So, who can you turn to for retirement advice before going where you have never gone before?

Yes, you might consult someone already retired, a friend or a neighbor. But is the friend or neighbor really going to open up about their net worth and personal finances? Is their idea of retirement a cruise in the Caribbean while yours is taking a rowboat out fishing at the lake? We all have different goals or aspirations.

Most people retire just once in their life unless they decide to have another career. As an accredited advisor, I help people dozens of times a year. What is more, I retired (to raise my kids) and came back. So, I have walked through it. I've seen the pitfalls. I know what can happen. I'm way more knowledgeable than the guy down the street or the girlfriend who is on welfare. I've been there, I've done that. That puts me in a unique position. How many advisors can say as much?

Another way to put it is that learning about retirement is like learning how to walk through a minefield. How would you learn to cross a field where the next step might be deadly?

You can talk to people, you can take courses, you can read books, you can join in a webinar, you can listen to a radio show.

But is there a better way to learn? You probably would try to find someone who walks through the minefield all the time. They know everything about the minefield. And then what they're going to do is tell you how to get through the minefield, take you by the hand and walk you through it and then walk behind you on the second trip while not allowing you to make a mistake. That's what retirement – or even learning how to drive on the freeway – is like.

I guide someone through the process probably twenty-five times a year. That's every other week. It is even more than that. Actually I have 500-plus clients and I check in with them regularly. I talk about retirement every day to clients one on one. Even after they retire, we're tinkering with their retirement plan. Yes, things change; we need to adjust.

I have not mentioned someone who decided to take the do-it-yourself approach. Might they not even be aware of mistakes they made? Might they have fallen behind inflation without even realizing it?

Every time I sit down with someone, I ask their risk tolerance. I ask them to answer my questionnaire. The section on personal investment attitudes measures their risk tolerance. There are about a dozen questions. Add up the points with zero being, I want to put my money in my mattress, and a hundred being a roulette wheel at Las Vegas.

Everybody is somewhere in between those extremes but most people are not aware where their comfort zone falls. So if you come to me and you've got a 401(k) and it's all in the stock market, which is invariably 70 to 100 on the risk scale, but your answers indicate *your* risk tolerance is about a 40, then we have a dichotomy going on. We have a fix to make.

Questionnaire

Filling out Kelley Slaught's questionnaire is a path to self-discovery for some prospective clients. It is a way to organize their financial assets, to articulate for the advisor their attitudes toward risk and investing, and think through what they want to do with their leisure time.

Date: ____________________

PERSONAL DATA

Name: ____________________
D.O.B.: ____________________ SS#: ____________________
DL#: ____________________ Occupation: ____________________
Company Name: ____________________
Expected Retirement Age: ____________________

Spouse: ____________________
D.O.B.: ____________________ SS#: ____________________
DL#: ____________________ Occupation: ____________________
Company Name: ____________________
Expected Retirement Age: ____________________

Name(s) and Age(s) of Children:
____
____

Address: ____________________
City: ____________________ State: _____ Zip: ________
Phone #: ____________________ Email: ____________________

HOUSEHOLD

Gross Annual Salary/Income: $ ____________________
Net Worth (Approx.)
Cash: $ ____________________
Stocks/MF: $ ____________________
Bonds: $ ____________________
IRA: $ ____________________
401K: $ ____________________
Life Insurance: $ ____________________ Term: ____________
Real Estate: $ ____________________
LTC: $ ____________________
Other/Collectibles: $ ____________________
Estimated State & Federal Tax Bracket: ____________________ %

PLEASE CIRCLE YOUR ANSWER

I have a need for income: Yes No $_________/mo.
I have the ability to save: Yes No $_________/mo.

PERSONAL INVESTMENT ATTITUDES

On a sale of 0 to 10 (0=Unimportant, 10=Most Important), how important are each of the following specific investment characteristics? Treat each category independently:

Safety of Principle/Income (0–10):______
Moderate Growth (0–10):______
Aggressive Growth (0–10):______
Speculation (0–10):______
High Current Income (0–10):______
Tax Liability Reduction (0–10):______

Please indicate the Preferred Risk Level which best describes the risk-reward relationship with which you are generally most comfortable. (Check only one): Limit ( ) Moderate ( ) Higher ( )

PERSONAL INVESTMENT GOALS

1. Are you planning for any major expenditures within:
1 year ( ) 3–5 years ( ) 5–10 years ( )
2. Are you planning to provide for your children's higher education?
Yes ( ) No ( )
3. Are you concerned with having adequate income during retirement?
Yes ( ) No ( )
4. Are you responsible for the financial welfare of anyone other than your immediate family (i.e., alimony, child support or parental support, etc.)?
Yes ( ) No ( )

Which of these **Personal Investment Goals** that you have answered *yes* to is ***MOST*** important to you? ______________________________

Which of these **Personal Investment Goals** that you have answered *yes* to is ***LEAST*** important to you? ______________________________

ADDITIONAL QUESTIONS

How did you hear about us? ______________________________

What scares or concerns you most about your portfolio? ______________

____

What is the most successful way for us to work together? ____________

____

Fixes need to be made with the work of do-it-yourselfers and even for clients transferring in with portfolios built elsewhere. Some new clients arrive with portfolios that are pre-made or by someone not in tune with their preferences or comfort zone. Or they went to a major brokerage but all their money is in the market. So yeah, I fix portfolios all the time. I adjust risk tolerances. I help them put some money in the market and some into safer investments.

Most people have no clue if some of the investments are inappropriate for them. They don't know what their tolerance is. They don't know how risky some investments are. They don't know that there are alternatives to the stock market that they can choose. I am happy to explain it to them.

A change in the industry, quite apparent after my child-raising break from active involvement, is this: Consumers and advisors *need not be* tied to some mega-brokerage or some firm limited to offering products from just one part of the investment spectrum.

Independent advisors today can readily purchase back-office services. The advisor is freed up to deal with the client and to craft a custom portfolio, not driven by sales quotas, institutionalized preferences of products and such.

It gives the consumer the best of both worlds: individual attention backed by professional recordkeeping, massive research databases and access to products from many companies.

I use a broker dealer for my back-office functions, as well as my personal office staff. I have clients across the nation and even in some foreign countries, as clients move or tell friends about my performance. Modern communications keep us in touch despite where life may take them.

A client, Allison from Texas, came to me a few years ago. She really wanted to retire. We looked at her funds and how much we could generate in income from them. It was not enough based on her budget of what she told me she needed in retirement.

I recommended she delay retirement or if she decided to go ahead that she get a part-time job to bring in needed income. She ultimately decided she wanted to retire and not get a part-time job.

So the funds we invested for her generated a certain amount of income but not enough to cover her full budgetary needs. We did leave about eighteen months' worth in cash that she could withdraw monthly to supplement the income we were generating. Those funds, I told her, would slowly deplete and she would run out of money. Then, we wouldn't have any cash left and we would have to start liquidating her investments. Eventually, the investments would run out as well.

She persisted. That is what she wanted to do.

So we invested some of the funds – not enough – to generate income. Some of the funds we left in cash to cover living expenses as needed.

Unfortunately, a year and a half went by and the cash was gone. The funds we had invested were still generating income but it wasn't enough to pay for her living expenses.

Allison went into a panic mode and really had some issues about how she was going to pay her bills.

Ultimately, we are liquidating the rest of her funds in order to pay her living expenses. But when she runs out of those funds there will be no money left for her.

My heart aches for a client like this who is living beyond her means and not doing anything about it.

Sadly, all I can do is make suggestions and recommendations. If clients refuse to follow what I recommend, they end up having extremely hard conversations with me and their loved ones about running out of money.

GETTING TO MEET YOU, GETTING TO KNOW YOU

I have clients all over the world. It is amazing how building relationships and helping people plan for successful retirements are rewarded with referrals.

Clients move around, they enjoy travel, they are pleased to be closer to grown children, they appreciate having medical facilities nearby. Home for many is not a forever concept, but the place where I live this year and maybe somewhere else the next.

California, and especially Santa Barbara, is where I was raised and where I nurtured my children. It is no surprise that I have a client base in Santa Barbara, Los Angeles and Orange County. People facing retirement everywhere need advice and help. It is no surprise that I have clients in Arizona, Texas, New York, and New Jersey, and other states as well. Yes, and some in China and Europe.

A client who is an attorney spends half the year on the East Coast, half the year on the West Coast. Wherever he goes, I am there for him. A famous opera singer is a client. She travels the world. We meet in person when we can or do Zoom meetings as she travels the world.

Modern communications can bring us together, no matter how many time zones or oceans away. The questions from clients or prospective clients or from my radio audience are similar.

It is fun doing a Saturday afternoon radio show. (KRLA, am 870, 8:00 to 9:00 a.m. and 3:00 to 4:00 p.m., Pacific time). I am sitting in my office, giant headphones on. I have my computer linked to my co-host, at another location. Yet the sound quality is so fine the listeners presume we are sitting right next to each other.

It takes time to establish a relationship, to build up trust in each other. Other hosts on this talk show station have become well known. So, I suspect that people listening to the premier episodes of my show hear my voice, the competence and what

I'm saying and the knowledge that I have. It goes a long way toward them feeling comfortable with working with me.

Feel free to join me Saturdays at 8:00 a.m. or 3:00 p.m. or listen to recordings of past shows. It's fun. Perhaps we will deal soon with the very question you have. If not, my website, https://www.Californiawealthadvisors.com/ tells how individuals can ask for a free consultation.

"I'm proud you've become a Doctor, son. You owe me $200,000 for medical school."

8

Lacking Understanding About Social Security and Medicare

Those government rules you have been ignoring for most of your life are about to slap you in the face.

I'm talking to you, the youngest of the Baby Boomers (people born 1946-1964). Meantime Millennials (1981-1996), back to your daily lives and retirement slumber.

Don't make the blunder of lacking a full understanding of Social Security and Medicare.

Be Aware Of Due Dates On Government Programs

The concept is that the government has age-based rules on privileges to help us get started in life such as student loans or ways to save tax-deferred for retirement. The "but" is that the government eventually wants its money back. The government also pushes us into mandatory programs with promises of benefits in the somewhat distant future. Social Security and Medicare are examples.

These programs can be incredibly complex with funding mechanisms changed from time to time to keep them from going broke. You can go about your daily life or yearly routine without giving them a thought. No matter except that now those long-promised benefits are on the horizon and ignorance no longer is bliss. There are forms to fill out, deadlines to meet and consequences if you don't.

What you don't understand about Social Security, Medicare, Required Minimum Distributions or retirement account conversions can harm you and your portfolio. Let's take the government programs one by one with just a few highlights and key dates to sear into your memory.

So You Think You Know Social Security

We all know about Social Security or at least think we do.

Many of us are not aware that income tax is collected on Social Security benefits (about 40 percent of recipients are taxed, the Social Security Administration estimates).

Some of us think that retirement begins at sixty-five. While early retirement with lower Social Security payouts can begin at age sixty-two, the age for full retirement payouts is now sixty-seven for people born in 1960 or later. That's right, if you are sixty-one or older, you must work until age 67 to collect normal benefits.

Younger generations are dubious that Social Security even will exist when it is their turn to collect benefits from a program they have paid into during their working careers.

Yes, there has been considerable and somewhat misunderstood news coverage about the pivotal year of 2035. That is when Social

Security, give or take two or three years either way and depending upon the agency doing the estimating, the trust fund is expected to run out of money. When that event occurs, however, it does not mean the program will come to a grinding halt. Instead, payouts are expected to continue but at reduced levels, perhaps 75 to 80 percent.22

The age when potential retirees should really pay attention is around 62. Delaying, instead of taking early retirement, can mean that benefits increase at a rate of 8 percent for every year until a cap is reached at age 70.

One in three persons who turn sixty-five this year, the Social Security Administration estimates, will live at least to ninety. Many may rue a decision to take early retirement with lower benefits for the rest of their lives if they begin taking Social Security too soon.

Still, there sometimes are compelling reasons to take early retirement. If you are in poor health with a short life expectancy, married late with dependents still in school now or have a seriously disabled child, early retirement may be in your best interest. Spouses with limited amounts of employment history face major decisions, particularly if the marriage ended in divorce or their partner has died.

The Social Security Administration has a retirement estimator which gives a rough approximation of what to expect and a more detailed calculator. The first step is to open a Social Security account which gives you access to your private career earnings (see www.SSA.gov).

Private organizations have calculators that use your general situation and an estimate of your average earnings. Since the formula is your thirty-five years of highest earnings and your pay tends to increase dramatically over your career, the calculation will necessarily be rough. (Even the Social Security Administration cannot provide a precise figure until you actually apply for benefits.)

Here is what AARP estimates for a single person, born in 1960 and earning a $50,000 salary:

$1,323 if retiring at age sixty-two.
$1,890 if retiring at age sixty-seven.
$2,344 if retiring at age seventy.

Or you can consult a wealth or retirement advisor, someone with professional training and refresher updates, and who typically does those calculations daily for potential clients.

Medicare Can Be A Mystery Too

Medicare is complicated, oh so complicated.

Medicare is designed for us to have reliable health care in place in retirement after we leave our employer's insurance umbrella. It is our hope to avoid catastrophic expenses and to have doctor bills that are manageable.

Yet Medicare itself is expensive, premiums are even higher for the well-to-do, it does not cover a lot of bills and there is no cap on what you may have to pay out.

Still, Medicare is a must.

Forgive me if I oversimplify on our path to dates to remember.

Medicare, Part A is for hospital bills. Medicare, Part B is for doctor bills. A and B are the standard package. But Medicare typically does not pay for prescriptions. So, Medicare, Part D, is for private insurance that consumers can purchase to cover those bills after the co-pays.

Medicare is not cheap. For 2021, a standard premium for Part B (medical services) is $148.50 a month yet those in higher tax brackets pay more, sometimes triple that. Costs also can vary from state to state. Typically, Medicare premiums are deducted from the amount of Social Security you receive.

What does Medicare not cover? One example is the "donut hole." Even if you are paying a private insurer for prescription coverage (Part D), bills incurred in one year are not covered from $4,130 to $6,550.

All in all, we know it is costly to get sick and that as people reach their senior years the bills are sure to mount. Fidelity Investments has been brave enough to issue a widely quoted estimate that a couple reaching sixty-five may need $295,000 during their later years for just basic medical and hospital expenses.[23]

Driving toward our dates to remember goal is that the three months before turning 65 and the four months afterward are critical when it comes to Medicare.

Six months before citizens turn sixty-five, the government sends out a catalog "Medicare & You." That should be a flag that a date the government deems important is coming. It should be to you, too.

Persons already drawing Social Security are automatically enrolled in Medicare. Persons covered by an employer's health plan and working past sixty-five – increasingly common – can wait to apply until the day that coverage stops. Procrastinate and you may experience a lapse in coverage and perhaps permanently higher premiums. I have a specialist I work with that helps people, for free, to figure out what medicare or supplemental insurance they need. I highly recommend you call me to get help you need.

Required Minimum Distributions

Tax-sheltered accounts allow untaxed savings to build, sometimes to large amounts, to help finance living when the paychecks stop. The government wants its money back, generally starting at a specific age and at a specified percentage withdrawal rate that increases as one ages. These are called Required Minimum Distributions or RMDs.

The age used to be the year in which one reached 70.5. The withdrawal requirement was suspended for 2020 because of COVID. It is back in place with a new starting age of seventy-two, and likely to increase more over the next ten years.

Money left in the account can continue to grow, sometimes faster than the size of the required distributions which are taxed. By the time a retiree reaches advanced age, however, the percentage of the account that must be withdrawn is quite high.

A retiree may have several retirement accounts held at different institutions. The minimum distribution is based on the total amount of tax-sheltered money and the total distribution can be taken from *any* account, not necessarily *each* account. The penalty for not withdrawing enough is quite severe.

Boy, is there a story here. I have a female client of means who had accounts with three firms and a certified public accountant responsible for preparing her taxes. On October 1 of last year, I checked in with her by phone about her portfolio and in particular this requirement.

Was she aware of how much in total she must withdraw?

She was.

Had she taken the year's minimum distribution?

Well, she was in the process of taking the full amount required from one of her bank retirement accounts.

I checked back on December 15. Had she taken out enough money to satisfy the government?

Oh yes, she was fine.

My phone rang on January 15.

There had been a miscommunication. What could she do?

"All you can do now is pay the penalty," I answered. "And perhaps you may want to have a frank talk with your CPA."

The penalty, as I said, is quite severe: 50 percent of the shortfall as well as taxes due on the amount of under-withdrawal.

The date to remember is well before the year ends.

Retirement Account Conversions

Roth IRAs are taxed before being put in an account. It will not be taxed again no matter how large it may grow.

Existing IRAs can be converted in part or in whole to Roth IRAs. This is a strategic decision for you to make. You should make an educated guess as to whether your income and tax rate are higher at the time of conversion or the time of withdrawal. The conversion makes sense if you anticipate being in a higher tax bracket later and then can withdraw tax-free.

The dates to remember here are the present and the future.

It is difficult enough to predict the future. Will you have to leave the work force suddenly and fall into a lower tax bracket? Will the government change the rules on Roth conversions? (Remember when Social Security benefits were not taxed?)

Perhaps this is a subtle suggestion that you should talk about such a move in advance with an advisor.

It is a given why I sit down with potential clients and discuss their present circumstances and their hopes and goals in retirement before formulating a plan.

There are age-based rules and deadlines in any financial deal made with the government, either by default or by choice. There are serious consequences for not complying with the terms of the deal. As retirement looms large in your future, you can try to go it alone or collaborate with an advisor.

There is a lot to be said for teamwork.

- The government has programs (student loans, retirement account tax shelters) to help us get toward retirement and long-promised benefits (Social Security, Medicare) for taxes paid along the way. There are deadlines and dates to remember, however.
- While lower Social Security benefits are available at age 62, one in three persons reaching age 65 is expected to live to 90. Will smaller monthly checks be enough?
- Standard Medicare consists of Part A (hospitalization) and Part B (doctors' services). Part D (prescription coverage) can be purchased through private companies.
- The key dates to remember on Medicare are three months before you turn 65 and the four months after.
- Required Minimum Distributions from tax-sheltered accounts now begin at age 72. Be sure to make the withdrawals before each year ends.
- Common IRAs, no tax due until retirement, can be converted into Roth IRAs, taxed up front and never again. The trick is, does it make sense to do a conversion?

PART III

What Comes Next

"I always hoped retirement would look like this."

9

Bonus Blunder: Set It and Forget It

Think of your doctor, think of your dentist. What would *they* say if they knew you hadn't even looked at your retirement plan in two years? Why, a review is painless – no drilling, no shots – and it could even make you money by making minor course adjustments to keep you on track to a stress-free retirement.

According to a survey by Voya Financial, 80 percent of those with retirement plans have avoided reviewing or making any changes over the previous year. That was compared to 43 percent of the respondents making changes to a phone, cable, or Internet plan.[24]

"Set it and forget it" is not a retirement strategy recommended by anyone. We work very hard collaborating on a custom retirement plan *designed just for you*. Yet change happens, sometimes in dramatic fashion, more often in very subtle ways. Remember as an adolescent the pained look on your face when visiting relatives would say, "My, how she has grown!" It was because they could see what your parents could not despite close daily contact.

A periodic review of your situation and your retirement plan is so important that I regularly check in with my clients. In between, I encourage them to call me if something has changed in their life.

A client should never set it and forget it. Investments are a changing/moving target. They go up and they go down in value. A retirement plan involves an investment strategy. It needs to be tweaked from time to time as the investing world changes. But more than the plan or strategy may need a minor course correction. Also in need of being monitored and reviewed with an advisor is *your* changing situation. People may have health issues, family issues and financial issues that have arisen since the plan was created. That may change what we should be doing in a portfolio. It may be as dramatic as a death of a spouse or receiving an inheritance. It may be as subtle as deciding you want to cover a grandchild's college education or to pay off debt.

Even if you think you have nothing to talk about during a periodic plan review, you probably do. Looking ahead, you may want to establish a family trust, complete with will, named beneficiaries, executor and designated individual to make the health directive decisions. What is more, it may be the right time to consolidate financial accounts from five financial institutions into one trusted firm. Upon your passing, that will raise confidence that all of the assets have been found. The executor thanks you in advance. What piece of mind can result from doing these administrative tasks while in good health.

The Society of Actuaries actually catalogued every type of risk/ change imaginable. You may never be so unlucky that you have to deal with most of these but the list does provide a framework of what might necessitate an adjustment. The items listed fall in three broad categories, personal and family, healthcare and housing, and financial.92

Employment risk. Employees may wish to work longer than the traditional retirement age but the decision is not up to them alone. Company downsizings and newer job skills being required are the norm today. Automation can transform the workplace. Part-time positions may be easier to find. John Wasik in Forbes.com cites a study by United Income that "Of Americans aged 65 or older and working or looking for work, 78 percent report being in good health or better, up from 73 percent in 1997 and 69 percent in 1985. As a result, more retirement-age people can work: 77 percent feel no limitations in the kind of work they can do, compared with 71 percent in 1997." [25]

Longevity risk. Outliving your money is a major fear in retirement. Longevity tables can tell you that based on your age today, what the typical life expectancy is. Add a few years if long lives run in the family, subtract a few or factor in higher medical bills if health issues exist.

Death of a spouse. Grief will affect your ability to make clear-headed decisions for a while. Income will decline as two Social Security checks drop to one. There are ways to protect income such as life insurance, survivors' pensions and partial long-term care policies. A retirement advisor and attorney can help with estate planning. I, like many independent retirement advisors, have a reciprocal referral relationship with a law firm.

Change in marital status. Separate living arrangements will mean a major hit to the standard of living for both partners. Two individuals living in their own homes will need about 20 percent more income, compared to those remaining in the same household, the Center for Retirement Research at Boston College estimates.[26]

Unforeseen needs of family members. Put yourself first so you don't become a burden to your family later, is the standard advice. "If oxygen use becomes necessary," the airlines tell us, "put your mask on first before helping others." Loaning your grown children money or helping with their financial mistakes, is a recipe for disaster. Financial planner Kristi Sullivan of Denver puts it this way: "For some people it's like taking an unexpected cruise every year with all of the expense and none of the fun." Put yourself first, yes, but what if it is your parent who needs to graduate to skilled nursing care and all of the siblings are being asked to chip in? This is where an emergency reserve fund may come into play.

Unexpected medical bills. Medicare is typically the major source of coverage. Yet Medicare only covers a portion of what the typical retiree must pay for medical expenses. AARP says original

Medicare A&B generally pays about 80 percent of what is billed in those categories. Prescription coverage (Part D) can be obtained from private companies but is paid by the recipient. Medicare Advantage plans offer broader coverage but have caps on what is paid out. AARP estimates about half of the expenses a retiree pays out of pocket are not reimbursed. According to a survey back in 2007, the median Medicare recipient was paying out of pocket $3,338. 95

Change in housing needs. You or your spouse may need assistance, either in performing daily living functions or skilled nursing. This may be sudden, as with a stroke or accident. Often, this can be foreseen with the passage of time. A plan review with your advisor may produce possible solutions.

Lack of caregivers. Sometimes, convenient care giving may not be available at any price. Rural isolation may be wonderful in the go-go years, not so much in the no-go years.

Inflation risk. People with do-it-yourself portfolios are most often in for an unpleasant surprise.

Interest-rate risk. Central banks for years have been keeping interest rates artificially low. A change if and when it comes will be a major adjustment.

Stock-market risk. Diversification is the antidote. It is a key part of my MAS Proprietary Process, dividing assets into three sectors plus an emergency reserve fund for the unexpected.

Business risks. These are less common but if the holder of your retirement assets goes bankrupt, the loss may not be fully covered or certainly a delay will occur in getting your money back.

Public policy risks. The government makes the rules on financial programs, the government can change them. You paid taxes on your earnings before they were put in the so-called Social Security pool. Now, when your money is being withdrawn, the government wants you to pay tax on it. Life is not fair. Public policy can change.

There are ways to anticipate and adjust to protect against these changes. Consulting with clients on retirement plan adjustments is a big part of the service I offer. Let's chat.

“How do the year end numbers look?”

10

Looking into Your Future

This book's focus so far has been on how to bring certainty to a very uncertain financial world and to create a retirement plan that leads to a successful entry into a wonderful new stage of life. We have looked, one construction phase at a time, at building that plan.

To be sure, it is a very uncertain financial world and quite unpredictable. Witness the Covid-19 pandemic that rocked all of us in so many ways. It drove us into isolation, took a horrid toll as it climbed toward 600,000 American deaths and millions more around the rest of the globe. It devastated the travel industry, large gatherings (the entertainment industry) and disrupted supply chains, creating barren grocery shelves. We had to eat but the pandemic ironically devastated restaurants everywhere.

Unemployment soared to double digits. Small businesses and even large ones such as Hertz could no longer continue business as they knew it. The pandemic disrupted all educational levels from kindergarten to grad school.

Who could have predicted that the near future would bring that?

And yet, never underestimate the resilience of Americans or the American economy. Modern medicine rushed to create vaccines, health officials worked without breaks to administer them. Some businesses adapted well, witness Zoom becoming a verb.

Through all of this, retirement planning went on. Some in the retirement Red Zone chose to turn a layoff or a business downturn into an earlier-than-planned retirement. Retirement advisors counseled others to cut living expenses, hunker down and wait a while for the inevitable economic rebound. "Hey, you have dreamed of traveling but you can't do that right now anyway."

I'd like to take a step back and view the big picture, one that is surprising bright from the retirement perspective. Yes, the financial world is unpredictable but some trends are clear – and relentless.

Let's look at some seemingly random threads and sew up the broader picture of what the future may bring.

Among these threads and a very bright outlook:

- A shift in the retirement planning industry as independent advisors farm out tedious back-office functions and do what they do best: consulting with and helping clients. Consumers will gain from ways to more efficiently manage their financial affairs and from exciting new products coming on-line.
- Social Security is still in crisis mode but it is *not* going away.
- We have sheltered at home, yes, but we are a mobile people and we will be on the move again. The pandemic showed that we can work from anywhere. The good news is that we can take our tax-sheltered accounts or convert them from anywhere as well.
- Government rules are not always rigid. Two significant changes to required minimum distributions from tax-sheltered accounts have made them more responsive to our needs.
- Perplexing problems are being targeted by industry experts and solutions will come. Long-term-care is barely available at any price? Look for new life insurance or annuity products to pop up. What to do about leaving money for a much younger spouse or a disabled child? We have answers.

- We don't age in a straight line nor does our spending. How to understand the three phases of retirement.

Consumers Win With New Choices, Better Rules

Industry trends. The retirement planning industry is changing. The goliaths are consolidating, as evidenced by Charles Schwab acquiring TD Ameritrade. Yet, an industry of 55,000 firms doing retirement planning or advice actually grew employment 3 percent from 2013. Independents are able to farm out recordkeeping and other back-office functions. They are able to do computer searches for what they consider the best deal on any given product. Consumers win.

Some aspects of the advisor-client relationship are more automated now – no doubt about it. Yet, what I find is that people want to have personal interaction with their financial advisor. Robo Advisors are great for some people who want to do everything themselves. However, when something happens via computer, you don't feel someone really knows you, your needs, your goals, your personal feelings about the investments you are in.

Have you ever negotiated the phone tree at some large firm, dealing with a robot? None of the options match what you are calling about. You persevere and try to explain, try to say who is calling. When you finally reach a human, none of the information has been passed forward and you are talking with someone who literally has no idea who you are. *Well, never at my firm.*

A personal relationship, especially with sensitive financial matters is so important. A computer cannot reassure you that help is available immediately when a spouse passes, when a medical issue arises, or other life challenges come your way.

People love people – they love the personal care I provide. I do care – deeply – for each of my clients. Clients become part of our family – and we care about them.

Social Security Trends

You've seen the headlines: the Social Security Trust Fund is going to be depleted sometime in the 2030s.[27]The year depends upon the agency making the estimate and when it was issued. Even worse, the trust fund that helps those with disabilities and Medicare's hospital insurance trust fund are expected to dry up in the 2020s.

Unless Congress gets around to acting.

What happens next? Social Security benefits will still be paid out but at a reduced rate. Currently Social Security is funded by a 12.4 percent payroll tax, split evenly between employees and employers. (The self-employed pay all of an even higher rate.) An AARP white paper estimates there will be sufficient incoming revenue to continue paying around three-fourths of scheduled benefits to retirees and survivors.[28]

We're On The Move

We have proven we can work at home, arguably even better. That goes the same for handling retirement matters.

We'll continue being on the move, from city to city or job-hopping from one employer to another. What happens to our company-related retirement accounts, the 401(k)s, their close cousins such as 403(b)s and even a lingering pension or two?

One choice is an IRA, or individual retirement account, which is quite portable. When you leave a company, you are usually given an option of leaving it with the 401(k) company as the manager or roll it into an IRA.

I always tell people *do not leave it there*. You have *many more* choices within your self-directed IRA than you would at your 401(k) – especially if you bring it to an independent financial firm like mine. Diversification is key – always. My MAS Proprietary Process is designed to take portfolios and create that diversification which gives peace of mind – rather than leave it in a 401(k) that will only be invested in the stock market.

Required Minimum Distributions. For decades the government has delayed taking its cut of money you earned but put into tax-sheltered accounts. Eventually, it wants its money. There is no escape save for paying the tax up front via a Roth IRA. This is about as rigid a government rule as you will find. Two decades went by without significant changes.

Until now. The pandemic forced a change in the age that withdrawals (Required Minimum Distributions) must be taken. It used to be around 70.5. Now it is in the year you turn seventy-two.

The life expectancy tables used to compute the size of the annual distribution had not been revised since 2002. Since then, life expectancy has increased more than 8 percent for Americans.

The formula for computing the amount the government is due is to take the year-end value in the account or accounts and divide by a life expectancy factor. The withdrawal amount must be paid by April 15, or a 50 percent penalty will be assessed on top of the shortfall.

The IRS says that 80 percent of Americans take out more than the required withdrawal anyway so they may notice little change.

Of three life expectancy tables used, the most common one is the Uniform Lifetime Table. The percentage withdrawal required increases with age. At 72 it is 3.67 percent based on a life expectancy factor of 27.3. The percentage that must be taken out goes up each year to 4.07 percent at age 75, 4.96 percent at age 80, 8.77 percent at age 90 and so forth.

Long-term-care

When a client needs long-term-care – the number one concern – we do have solutions. However, a straight long-term-care policy can cost as much as $30,000 to $40,000 per year and if you pass away the next day, there's nothing left.

Rather than do that, we have three different solutions:

1. Purchase a life insurance policy that has LTC as part of the policy. We will run illustrations for people based on their birthday, health, etc. The numbers we will provide them with the illustration will show a multiplied death benefit (tax free benefit to their heirs), a long-term-care monthly benefit, and

income streams that can be generated (tax free) if the client does not use the LTC. A popular choice by clients is premiums of $10,000 to $20,000 per year for 10 years. This allows the engine to grow within the life insurance and creates cash value if the client ever wants to liquidate the policy altogether.

2. I can take an old life insurance policy that has cash value built up and do a 1035 exchange into a new life insurance policy that has LTC. We make it a much better policy that actually works for the client and gives them some much-needed benefits. Sometimes clients come to me, and their life insurance premium is just about to increase exponentially. To avoid large increases like that, we do the 1035 tax-free exchange into a better life insurance policy.

3. If a client does not qualify for life insurance due to health issues, we do have annuities that have long-term-care options available. They don't have to go through the underwriting process that life insurance requires, so we can get these set up for clients who need that.

I have a client that wanted a life insurance policy with LTC. Once we did the underwriting, due to his health issues, he did not qualify. So, instead we did an annuity for him with the focus on LTC. He is very happy and secure in the knowledge that he has LTC if he ever needs it.

Perplexing Problems

How to plan for a much younger spouse or a disabled child? It is best to consult with a retirement advisor. A different life expectancy table can be used, providing a break for a spouse ten years or younger. An annuity or a trust fund are possibilities for a disabled child.

Retirement can best be divided into three stages: the go-go years, the slow-go years and the no-go years.

Who said that? Financial planner Michael Stein in his 1998 book, *The Prosperous Retirement: Guide to the New Reality.*[29]

The go-go years are typically up to age seventy-five. Retirees may be done working although it is increasingly common to have a part-time job. They have the time and energy to travel, volunteer and pursue hobbies with gusto. Their spending tends to reflect that.

The slow-go years are from seventy-five to eight-five. Life centers on the familiar and becomes more routine. The body may slow and the urge to travel may fade. More time is spent at home and spending may decline.

The no-go years generally are from eighty-five onward. Retirees' mobility and activity may decline sharply. Spending may decrease unless major illnesses occur or force a move to a retirement home or assisted living facility.

Stein's major points are that spending may – repeat may – take a somewhat counter-intuitive drop and that non-financial quality of life adjustments may be necessary as aging progresses.

His thesis on spending has been borne out by research although printed surveys are infrequent.

Consider a Consumer Expenditure Survey by the US Bureau of Labor Statistics. It was done in September 2015 so don't expect to find the same prices today, especially in the inflation-prone healthcare category. A table below shows the percentage of significant spending for selected items in the 55-64, 65-74 and 75-plus demographics.

Average total expenditures – back then – were \$56,267, \$48,885 and \$36,673. Instead of spending numbers, the percentages of total retiree spending are used in the table here. With declining activity, food consumed away from home dropped irregularly from 4.8 percent to 5.3 percent to 3.8 percent. Transportation showed a similar pattern going from 16.6 percent to 17.1 percent to 13.9 percent.

Retiree Household Spending By Age

(expressed as percentage of total household spending)

CATEGORY	55-64	65-74	75 AND UP
Food at home	7.3	7.6	8.0
Food away	4.8	5.3	3.8
Housing	32.0	32.4	36.5
Transportation	16.6	17.1	13.9
Healthcare	8.8	12.2	15.6
Entertainment	5.1	6.1	4.4
Cash contrib.	3.4	4.4	8.1

This is a rough guide to typical spending in retirement. Of course, we have another rough or base-line gauge of spending – where our money went during our final working years. Some categories such as commute costs, business attire and retirement account contributions may decline.

Your monthly spending needs will be among the first questions your advisor asks in the interview process.

Remember, there is always something to be bullish about.

Budget

	BUDGET AMOUNT	ACTUAL AMOUNT	DIFFERENCE
INCOME			
Regular Income			
Wages & Bonuses			
Interest Income			
Investment Income			
Misc. Income			
Income Subtotal			
Income Taxes Withheld			
Federal Income Tax			
State & Local Income Tax			
Social Security/Medicare Tax			
Income Taxes Subtotal			
Spendable Income			
EXPENSES			
Home			
Mortgage or Rent			
Homeowners/Renters Insurance			
Property Taxes			
Home Repairs/Maintenance/HOA			
Home Improvements			

Utilities			
Electricity			
Water & Sewer			
Natural Gas or Oil			
Internet (Phone/Computer)			
Food			
Groceries			
Eating Out, Lunches, Snacks			
Family Obligations			
Child Support			
Day Care, Babysitting			
Health & Medical			
Insurance (Medical/Dental)			
Out-of-Pocket Medical			
Fitness (Yoga/Massage/Gym)			
Transportation			
Car Payments			
Gasoline/Oil			
Auto Repairs/Car Maintenance			
Auto Insurance			
Other (Bus, Taxi, Subway)			
Debt Payments			
Credit Cards			
Student Loans			
Other Loans			

Entertainment/Recreation			
Hobbies			
Subscriptions & Dues			
Vacations			
Videos & Movies			
Pets			
Food			
Grooming			
Clothing			
Investments & Savings			
401(K)/IRA			
Stocks/Bonds/Mutual Funds			
College Fund			
Savings			
Emergency Fund			
Miscellaneous			
Toiletries/Household Products			
Gifts/Donations			
Grooming (Hair, Make-up, Other)			
Misc. Expense			
Total Investments & Expenses			
SURPLUS/SHORTAGE (Income minus Expenses)			

Asset Sheets

The following data is strictly confidential. The information will be analyzed by one of financial planners and you may receive a personalized financial plan which will answer important questions listed on the cover. The written plan may also include recommendations or specific investments and other financial planning tools that you should consider to help you meet your family's needs and achieve your goals.

Instructions for purpose of identification. List the individual with the larger annual income as **Client A**. The individual with the lesser income, or a non-working spouse, should be listed as **Client B**. When entering figures use only dollar amounts. Do not enter cents. If you are unable to complete some sections, or have questions, write ***please call*** in the margin and you financial planner will consult with you prior to developing your financial plan.

1. PERSONAL DATA

Today's Date ______________

A. Personal Data: First Name M.I. Last Name	Age	Sex	Birth Date	Social Sec. #
Client A				
Client B				
Dependents (See Planned Children below):				College Funding**
Oldest Child				
Child 2				
Child 3				
Child 4				
Child 5				
Other Dependent & Relationship				
Other Dependent & Relationship				

*PLANNED CHILDREN. If you plan to have children, or additional children, please write *planned* in the dependent space and indicate the approximate planned birth date.

**COLLEGE FUNDING If you anticipate paying for your children's college education, write *yes*. You may specify an amount to educate in today's dollars. If you do not specify an amount, we will use the average state college figure.

B. HOME ADDRESS Home Phone ( ) -	**D. EMPLOYMENT DATA**
Street	**Client A:** self-employed? ☐ Yes ☐ No
City State Zip	Occupation:
Client A Business Phone ( ) -	Employer: ______ Years
Client B Business Phone ( ) -	**Client A:** self-employed? ☐ Yes ☐ No
C. PRO. ADVISORS **Name/Firm** **Telephone**	Occupation:
Accountant ( ) -	Employer: ______ Years
Attorney ( ) -	Do you smoke cigarettes? **Client A** ☐Y ☐N **Client B** ☐Y ☐N

2. GOALS AND ASSUMPTIONS

The following information is necessary in order to develop a plan that, when implemented, will reflect your expectations for the future, meet your needs, and be consistent with your temperament, goals and objectives.

A. YOUR INVESTMENT ATTITUDE

Generally, people can afford to be more aggressive and assume risks while young, but should be more conservative when close to retirement.

Client A (circle one) 1 2 3 4 5 6 7 8 9 10

Client B (circle one) 1 2 3 4 5 6 7 8 9 10

B. DESIRED INVESTMENT FEATURES

Rank the following from 1-4 in order of importance accordingly to your present situation, with 1 indicating the most important feature.

____ Liquidity ____ Current Income ____ Growth ____ Tax-Advantage*

*Tax-Advantage - Refers to lowering your present income taxes through deferrals or deductions, creating tax-free income.

C. ASSUMED AVERAGE ANNUAL INFLATION RATE (If other than 7%) ______ %

Since the early 1970's, we have experienced a sustained period of inflation, averaging over 7% per year since 1973. This has been an uncharacteristic period in our nation's history, yet sound financial planning dictates that we base today's plans on a figure that would properly prepare an individual for the future should we again experience high inflation. We will base our calculations on a 7% annual rate unless you specify a greater or lesser rate in the space above.

D. PLANNED RETIREMENT AGE ________

E. MONTHLY GROSS INCOME DESIRED AT RETIREMENT (Pre-Tax, in Today's Dollars) $ ________

Carefully estimate what it would take to meet your basic living expense during retirement, and to fund your desired discretionary expenses, such as recreation and travel.

F. SOCIAL SECURITY Do you want to use Social Security as part of your retirement benefits? ☐Y ☐N

3. CASH BALANCES

Name of Institution: Also specify whether Bank, S&L, Credit Union, or Money Market Fund
Type: Checking Account = CK; Passbook Savings = PS; Certificate of Deposits = CD; Money Market = MM

Name of Institution	Type	$ Current Balance	Interest Rate %		
				Period	$ Amount/Period

4. OTHER ASSETS

Type: Mutual Funds = MF; Stock = S; Corporate Bonds = CB; Government or Muni. Bonds = GB; Annuities = A;
Real Estate Limited Partnerships or Trusts = RE; Oil & Gas Partnerships = OG; Other Tax Shelters = TS

INVESTMENT		Owner A or B	CURRENT		ADDITIONS	
NAME	TYPE		Shares	$ Estimated Value	Period	$ Amount/Period

5. IRAs, 401Ks, ETC.

Type: Mutual Funds = MF; Stock = S; Corporate Bonds = CB; Government or Muni. Bonds = GB; Annuities = A;
Real Estate Limited Partnerships or Trusts = RE; Oil & Gas Partnerships = OG; Other Tax Shelters = TS Plan: IRA = I; SEP = SEP; 401K = K

INVESTMENT		Plan I or K	Owner A or B	CURRENT		ADDITIONS	
NAME	TYPE			Shares	$ Estimated Value	Period	$ Amount/Period

6. EMPLOYER SPONSORED RETIREMENT PLANS

Plan Type	$ Current Value (lump sum)	$ Monthly Benefits Expected (if know)	$ Current Death Benefit (to beneficiary)	ADDITIONS	
				Period	$ Amount/Period
Pension (Client A)					
Pension (Client B)					
TSA (Client A)					
TSA (Client B)					
Profit Sharing (Client A)					
Profit Sharing (Client B)					

7. REAL ESTATE PORTFOLIO DETAIL

Type of Property	Owner A/B & %	$ Market Value	$ Mortgage Value	$ Monthly Pymt. (Price & Int.)	Interest Rate %	$ Equity	$ Property Taxes
1. Home (1st Mortgage)							
Home (2nd Mortgage)							
2. Recreation Property*							
Investments or Rental Properties**							

*Indicate if a balloon payment will be paid and due date.
**Do not enter here any property taxes in the calculations of Net Rental Income in the Income Data Section.

8. BUSINESS ASSETS

	Description	Owner A/B & %	$ Present Value/Balance	$ Net Annual Income/Payments	Loan Rate %
Business					
Tangible Assets*					
Money Owed You					

*Tangible Assets Investment items not considered as personal property, such as gold and silver bullion or coins, investment quality diamonds, and other collectibles.

9. INCOME SOURCES

A. Present Income (Pre-tax)	$ Client A	$ Client B	**B. Anticipated Income**	20____	20____
1. Salary/Wages and Bonus			13. Combined Salary & Bonus (Client A &B)		
2. Net Income from Self-Employment			14. Combined Self-Employment (Client A &B)		
3. Interest Income			15. Interest Income		
4. Dividends			16. Dividends		
5. Capital Gains (sale of stock, real estate, etc.)			17. Capital Gains (sale of stock, real estate, etc.)		
6. Net Rental Income (excluding depreciation)			18. Net Rental Income (excluding depreciation)		
7. Trusts			19. Trusts		
8. Social Security Benefits			20. Social Security Benefits		
9. IRA/401K/KEOUGH Distributions/Withdrawals			21. IRA/401K/KEOUGH Distributions/Withdrawals		
10. Pensions/Military Retirement			22. Pensions/Military Retirement		
11. Other (Money Owed You, Etc.)			23. Other (Money Owed You, Etc.)		
12. Total Present Income	$	$	**24. Total Present Income**	$	$

10. INCOME TAX DATA

A. Filing Status (check one) ☐ Married ☐ Single ☐ Head of Household ☐ Married/Separately

B. Estimated Taxable Income (Current Year)	Section	$ Amount
1. Total Present Income (from above)	9	$
2. Non-taxable Income (e.g., Social Security, exempt interests, etc.)		( )
3. 401K / SEP Deduction		( )
4. Other Adjustments		( )
5. Modified Adjusted Gross Income (Line 1 minus Lines 2,3 & 4)		$
6. IRA Deductions and Standardized Itemized Deductions		( )
7. Exemptions		( )
8. Family Net Taxable Income (Line 5 minusLines 6 & 7)		$

C. Total Taxes Paid Last Year: **Federal $** ____________ **State $** ____________ **FICA $** ____________

11. INSURANCE

Insurance Company Name	Type	Insured A or B	Beneficiary A, B Other	$ Face Amount	$ Cash Value	$ Loans Against	Loan Int. Rate %	Annual Premium
	Group Term	Client A						
	Group Term	Client B						

After you have completed the above summary, fill out the insurance Policy Receipt Form. When you return this data form, enclose your Life & Disability Insurance policies and any other policies you would like your planner to review in the envelope provided. It will be very difficult for your planner to accurately analyze your insurance program without these policies.

12. DETAIL OF ASSETS

The Sec Column indicates which Detail Section has the information needed to complete this line.
EPRR% is the Estimated Pre-Tax Rate of Return in percent. However, if you are unsure of a number (such as Rate of Return), you may estimate it and your planner may provide the amount for you.

A. ASSETS	Sec	$ Current Value/Balance	EPRR%	15. Pension, Profit Sharing, TSA Value/Balance	6		
1. Checking Account	3			16. IRA, SEP	5		
2. Savings Accounts (Banks, S&L, Credit Union)	3			17. 401K	5		
3. Money Market Fund (taxable)	3			18. Tax Shelters & Limited Partnerships	4		
4. Total Cash (add lines 1, 2 & 3)	$			19. Tax Shelters & Limited Partnerships	7		
5. Home (market value)	7			20. Money Owed You	8		
6. Personal Property				21. Other Assets	8		
7. Personal Assets (add lines 4,5 & 6)	$			22. Investment Assets (ADD Lines 8 thru 22)	$		
8. Certificates of Deposits	3			22. Investment Assets (ADD Lines 7 & 22)	$		
9. Life Insurance Cash Value	11			**B. LIABILITIES**	Sec	Current Balance	
10. Annuities	4			24. Home Mortgage (balance)	7		
11. Stocks	4			25. Long-term Loans (3 years or more)			
12. Bonds (Corp. & Gov.)	4			26. Short-term Debts (under 3 years)			
13. Mutual Funds	4			27. Personal Liabilities (LINE 24, 25 & 26)	$		
14. Tangible Assets (investments)	8			28. Real Estate Mort. (other than home)	7		
*NOTE: Line 6 includes home furnishings, autos, boats, etc. Antiques, heirlooms, jewelry, silver place settings, stamp collection, etc. that you do not want to sell, and should be considered personal items. Investment items, such as gold and silver bullion or coins, investments quality diamonds, and other collectibles, should be included in the Tangible Assets figure, Line 14)				29. Loan Against Insurance Cash Value	11		
				30. Loans or Debts Secured by Investments	4		
				31. Investment Liabilities (ADD Lines 28, 29 & 30)	$		
				32. Total Liabilities (Lines 27 & 31)	$		

13. MONTHLY CASHFLOW

The Sec Column indicates which Detail Section has the information needed to complete this line.
NOTE: If some costs occur in periods other than monthly, first calculate the amount paid yearly. Then divide by 12.

A. Savings & Investments	Sec	$ Monthly	B. Taxes	Sec	$ Monthly	D. Standard of Living	$ Monthly
1. Savings Account			10. Federal Income Taxes (estimated for current year)			23. Housing-Mortgage payments (principal & interest) or rent	
2. Money Market Fund			11. State Income Taxes (estimated current year)			24. Auto/Trans. (gas, maint., payments)	
3. IRA			12. FICA - Social Security (estimated for current year)			25. Debt Repayment (credit cards, other loans)	
4. 401K			13. Property Taxes (personal residences)	7		26. Food (Home or Work)	
5. Pension Plans, TSA			14. Other ______			27. Medical/Dental (uninsured or no-ins.)	
6. Mutual Funds			15. Total Taxes	$		28. Entertainment/Recreation	
7. Stocks, Bonds, etc.			**C. Insurance**	Sec	$ Monthly	29. Education	
8. Other ______			16. Life Insurance	11		30. Charity, Gifts	
9. Total Savings & inv.	$		17. Disability Insurance	15		31. Clothing	
Are you currently following a systemic savings plan? ☐Y☐N			18. Health/Dental Insurance			32. Vacation	
If so, what are your monthly contributions? $ ______			19. Homeowner's/ Renter's Insurance			33. Home Maintenance/ Furnishings	
			20. Auto Insurance			34. Utilities & Misc. (phone, newspaper, etc.)	
			21. Other ______			35. Unreimbursed Employee Benefits	
			22. Total Insurance	$		36. Other ______	
						37. Total Standard/Living	

14. BUDGET NEEDS IF REQUIRED

In today's economy the death of either spouse can cause considerable financial hardship. Therefore, it is important that you project needs for an individual or spouse and family in the event of either spouse's death. Use today's dollars.

A. IMMEDIATE CASH REQUIREMENTS (In the event that either spouse dies today)	Section	NEEDS OF CLIENT B (If Client A dies)	NEEDS OF CLIENT A (If Client B dies)
1. Financial Expenses & Cash Reserve (The amount needed for Funeral Services and Burial, and to pay current bills for 3 months)			
2. Home Mortgage If there is mortgage insurance on either or both spouses, or if you wish to completely pay off any mortgage upon the death of either spouse, list the amount here. Otherwise, consider the monthly payment as part of the surviving spouse's monthly income needs below.			
3. Long-term Loans 3 Years of more (auto, boat, etc.) that you wish to pay-off immediately.			
4. Short-term Loans Under 3 years (credit cards, etc.) that you wish to pay-off immediately.			
B. INCOME & EXPENSES			
1. For Surviving Spouses & Children Until Youngest Reaches Age 16 (Families without dependent children, or with no plans for children, use these lines. Your figures will represent monthly income requirements now)			
Monthly Expenses			
Monthly Earned Income			
3. For Surviving Spouse During Retirement			
Monthly Expenses			
Monthly Earned Income - for example, from part-time work (Do no include anticipated income from Social Security of investments)			

15. DISABILITY REQUIREMENTS

A. Standard of Living If you become disabled today, how much of your monthly income Would you need to replace in order to maintain your family's standard of living? Client A $ ______ Client B $ ______

B. EXISTING COVERAGE	Insurance Company	Monthly Benefits	Waiting Periods	MAX Benefit Period	$ Annual Premium
Through Employer, Client A					
Through Employer, Client B					
Personally, Client A					
Personally, Client B					

16. WILL INFORMATION

	Client A	Client B
Do you have a current will?	☐ YES ☐ NO	☐ YES ☐ NO
When did you last review your will?		
Type of will (check one):	☐ Simple, All to SurvivingSpouse ☐ Two-part Martial Deduction	☐ Simple, All to Surviving Spouse ☐ Two-part Martial Deduction
If you have another trust describe:		

17. OTHER GOALS AND NEEDS

1. Amount, if any (in today's dollars) for your estimate at your natural life expectancy. $ ______

2. The goal of financial planning and investing is not simply to help you achieve financial independence at retirement. In many cases, a financial planner can design a program for you, which takes into account special considerations or needs other than retirement income. List any short or long terms goals or needs you may have which will affect your finances (e.g. new home purchases, travel, healthcare/medical, business). Designate short-term (within 5 years) or long-term (more than 5 years). Indicates special interests in specific investments you may want us to consider when analyzing your needs and developing your plan.

Acknowledgments

There are many people that have helped me in my career and thank you all. I'd especially like to thank my marketing team, headed by SD and KP, for encouraging me to write this book.

About the Author

Chances are if you wanted a partner for a tennis doubles match, you would choose Kelley Slaught. Chances are if you wanted someone in your golf foursome to show you, by example, how to replace some golf frustration with some golfing fun that brings you back for more, you would choose Kelley Slaught.

The CEO and owner of California Wealth Advisors is as home in the business suite as the tennis court or the golf course.

The daughter of a teaching tennis pro, she started playing at age five and switched to golf at age thirty. She found that in all three venues drive and setting goals lead to success.

Kelley, whose dad thought the extra E was more feminine, attended Idaho State and UC Irvine on tennis scholarships, then graduated from UC Santa Barbara.

After a week in an entry-level job at then Dean Witter she set her sights and drive on becoming a financial advisor. Eight years later, she took time out from her advisor role to raise three children, now in their twenties. It was a decision that she feels makes her uniquely qualified to discuss retirement. "Hey, I was 'retired' in a sense."

Kelley formed her own company in 2012. She says don't let the name California Wealth Advisors fool you. She has clients across the nation.

If you have a retirement question, especially one that is generic and of interest to many others, one way to reach her is at Kelley@californiawealthadvisors.com. If there are so many requests that she personally cannot answer each one, she will try to share via other forums, her website at https://wwwcaliforniawealthadvisors.com, her 8 a.m. and 3 p.m. (PT) Saturday KRLA radio show, or even a future webinar.

Kelley Slaught offers securities and advisory services through Centaurus Financial Inc., member FINRA/SIPC, a registered investment advisor. Centaurus Financial, Inc. and California Wealth Advisors are not affiliated companies. The opinions expressed are not intended to be a recommendation or investment advice and does not constitute a solicitation to buy, sell or hold a security or an investment strategy. The views and opinions expressed in this book are for information and educational purposes only.

Endnotes

1 https://www.aarp.org/work/job-search/info-2020/part-time-jobs-for-re..., accessed May 12, 2021

2 https://www.pewresearch.org/fact-tank/2019/07/24/baby-boomers-us...,accessed May 13, 2021

3 https://www.forbes.com/advisor/retirement/fixed-index-annuity/, "What Is A Fixed Index Annuity?", David Rodeck, Forbes, accessed May 3, 2021.

4 https://www.forbes.com/advisor/retirement/fixed-index-annuity/, "What Is A Fixed Index Annuity?" , David Rodeck, Forbes contributor, accessed May 3, 2021.

5 Adam Hayes "Financial Markets: When Fear and Greed Take Over," Investopedia. https://www.investopedia.com/articles/01/030701.asp, accessed May 1, 2021

6 Kristina Zuchi. "How to Avoid Emotional Investing," Investopedia. https://www.investopedia.com/articles/basics/10/how-to-avoid-emotional-investing.asp, accessed May 1, 2021

7 Lawrence E. Lipson and Richard A. Geist, *The Psychology of Investing*. New York: Wiley, 1999.

8 https://www.aarp.org/money/investing/info-2020/lessons-from...recessions-html Jane Bryant Quinn, accessed May 6, 2021

9 Sources: The Vanguard Study: In February 2019, Vanguard published research that attempted to quantify the benefits that advisors can add by providing cogent wealth management through financial planning, discipline, and guidance. According to Vanguard's report, "Putting a value on your value: Quantifying Vanguard Advisor's Alpha," this framework can add about 3% in net returns for clients. Additional sources: https://www.fidelity.com/viewpoints/investing-ideas/financial-advisor-cost; https://aon.mediaroom.com/news-releases?item=136959

10 https://www.aarp.org/money/investing/info-2019/stock-lessons-marke..., accessed May 6, 2021

11 https://www.covenantwealthadvisors.com/poststock-market-timing-2020-important-lessons, accessed May 6, 2021

12 https://www.forbes.com/sites/jimwang/2020/03/06/6=reasons-why-m...,accessed May 6, 2021

13 https://www.cnbc.com/2021/03/24/this-chart-shows-investors-...,accessed May 6, 2021

14 https://www.fool.com/investing/2021/04/30/stop-trying-to-time-market-and-do-this-instead/, accessed May 6, 2021

15 Fisher Investments booklet, "13 Retirement (Investment) Blunders to Avoid." Fisher Investments.

16 https://www.forbes.com/advisor/investing/what-is -diversifacation/Rob Berger and Benjamin Curry, accessed May 4, 2021

17 https://www.investopedia.com/ask/answers/12/inflation-interest-rate-relationship.asp, accessed May 20, 2021

18 Ryan Dezember, Georgi Kantchey, and Chulin-Wei Yap. "Commodities Remain a Popular Bet Despite Recent Declines," *The Wall Street Journal*, June 27, 2021.

19 https://www.thebalance.com/core-inflation-rate-3305918, accessed May 20, 2021

20 https://www.aarp.org/retirement/social-security/info-2020/colas-history, accessed May 20, 2021.

21 https://www.Broadcastingexperts.com, accessed May 21, 2021

22 Bob Carlson. "Social Security Trust Fund Expected To Run Dry Three Years Earlier Than Expected A Few Months Ago," Forbes.com, Oct. 24, 2020.

23 Social Security Calculator," AARP, updated June 2020, accessed March 25, 2021, www.aarp.org/retirement/social-security/benefits-calculator.html

24 https://www.money.usnews.com/investing/articles/2017-01-06/3-reasons-... accessed May 25, 2021

25 John Wasik in Forbes.com. https://www.forbes.com/sites/johnwasik/2019/06/03/why-working-pas-retirement-age-may-make-sense/?=31fba2afa799, accessed May 25, 2021

26 https://www.investopedia.com/articles/retirement/08/[post-retirement-... Accessed May 25, 2021

27 Stephen C. Goss, "The Future Financial Status of the Social Security Program." Social Security Bulletin, Vol. 70, No. 3, 2010.

28 https://www.aarp.org/content/dam/aarp/research/public_policy_institute/health/who-relies-on-Medicare-factsheet-AARP-ppi-health.pdf, accessed May 25, 2021

29 Michael Stein. *The Prosperous Retirement: Guide to the New Reality*. Emstco Pr, 1998